Dialogue with
a Somnambulist

ALSO BY CHLOE ARIDJIS

Sea Monsters

Asunder

Book of Clouds

Dialogue with a Somnambulist

STORIES, ESSAYS & A PORTRAIT GALLERY

•

Chloe Aridjis

WITH AN INTRODUCTION BY

TOM McCARTHY

CATAPULT   NEW YORK

First Catapult edition: 2023

ISBN: 978-1-64622-182-0

Library of Congress Control Number: 2023931311

Jacket design and illustration by Nicole Caputo

Catapult
New York, NY
books.catapult.co

Printed in the United States of America

1 3 5 7 9 10 8 6 4 2

Contents

The Limned Route
by Tom McCarthy — xiii

***

Stories

*

Essays

*

Portrait Gallery

*

***

The Limned Route

'The space between', muses the heroine of Ann Quin's novel *Three*, 'is no less significant than the place occupied at the time.' The statement is a kind of one-line manifesto, laying out a credo that is at once spatial, psychoanalytical, political and, above all, literary. If this credo has a contemporary advocate, it's Chloe Aridjis.

Born to the Mexican son of a wandering Greek and the expat Jewish daughter of second-generation immigrant New Yorkers; raised in a set of transfers between Manhattan, The Hague and Bern; steeped in French literature in New England and English subculture in Mexico City; writing in English albeit brought up bilingual – Aridjis not only, in her very person, embodies transposition, translation and general slippage but also, in her work, spins a whole delicate aesthetic around these. The world of both her fiction and her essays is made up of porous, endlessly shifting borders, interstices, zones that hover between cities, between languages and cultures, sleep and waking, the actual and the artificial, life and death. Characters are never fully 'present', but rather glimpsed in passing as they disappear down alleyways, or hidden by pseudonyms and false identities, or displaced onto strange objects – circus fleas, sea monkeys or a wax avatar that, in turn, melts. Territories are never laid out plainly, mapped and navigable: they, too, are (like the oil paintings of Aridjis's novel *Asunder*) scrambled by fissures, fault-lines that make labyrinths of their surfaces. Like a hacker who has landed a job with an ordnance-survey company, Aridjis's impulse, even as she explores a subject, is to sabotage the cartographic project she's signed up to. That's why the insomniac heroine of 'In the Arms of Morpheus', having enrolled in a sleep-study clinic, storms out when its director informs her that the 'data' 'proves' that 'dreams are nothing more than electrical discharges' – but not before asking for the name of a male co-patient she briefly caught sight of in the waiting room, then slept a few feet away from, separated by a curtain. Unsuccessfully: confidentiality rules prevent the doctors from disclosing this; which act of occlusion allows the image of the man to haunt her well into the future, as she lies, still a denizen of sleeplessness's limbo, next to a snoring husband whom the spectre both inhabits and displaces.

As for inner space, so, too, for outer: 'Into the Cosmos', nominally an essay but in essence as poetic as any of the fictions, moves from a West Berlin circus adaptation of Bulgakov's *The Master and Margarita* to East Berlin's Allee der Kosmonauten, then onwards to the history of Soviet cosmonauts, and Soviet circus, and thence (via their shared propensity for gravity-defiance) to Jarry, Baudelaire and Kleist, each context offsetting the other, before culminating in the glorious coda:

> How to map this darkness? One might argue that
> in the end both outer space and inner space are

destined to remain shrouded in mystery and ultimately unknowable – and unconquerable. We may undertake new voyages, assign coordinates, put names to the visible and the invisible, yet it is elusive territory to which we simply give form and measurement; wherever he finds himself, man's impulse is to limn his own mortal routes.

Limn is a lovely word. It sounds like it should come from *limen*, threshold, and pertain to everything that's liminal, in-between – but in fact it comes from *lumen*, light, and refers to the illumination of manuscripts or the embellishing with gold of icons and reliefs, as in Mexican churches. That Mexico, its history, has been both limned and rent asunder by gold is not lost on Aridjis: it's the starting point for the reflections contained in another essay piece, 'Baroque'. For her, Mexico is pure liminality, 'pivotal overlap', fluidity, exuberance; a 'syncretic' overlay of European and pre-Columbian civilisations that enacts 'a constant play between veiling and unveiling'; a melting and morphing territory whose art has always 'rejected straight lines and predictable paths, revelling in a liberated geometry' and in the moves of whose popular wrestlers the 'boundary' between performer and audience is broken, 'the geometry of the ring is defied, its quadrangle stretched and deformed again and again'. Most illuminating, though, is that the most detailed portrait that Aridjis gives us of a Mexico City resident is a supra-documentary study (titled 'Map of a Lost Soul') of a displaced German woman who, abandoned by her family while visiting many years ago, has been wandering the city in a fugue state ever since. This, Aridjis seems to want to tell us, is the truth of

Mexico: it's all fugue, all displacement. That's why, in 'The Tension of Transience' (where the term *baroque* appears again), the city's goth clubbers, via clothes bought in a Berlin warehouse, channel Victorian English mourning dress and Caspar David Friedrich paintings while they dance to Ultravox and snog with Scottish DJs – before, out in the car park, stray bullets cut fresh geometries across the air above their heads, heralding a new 'baroque', an approaching era of exuberant excess in which cartels will reprise, or syncretise, the sacrificial rituals of the Aztecs and the barbarism of conquistadors, out-grotesqueing Goya as they hang limbs from bridges and toss heads out onto dance floors.

Yet Mexico, for Aridjis, is less a place than a state of mind, a condition. Observing London, where she now lives, she spots similar displacements, similar fugues, similar veils and disappearances – and, in the brutal rapacity of the current regime, the massive pandemic death toll to which its incompetence and kleptocracy have given rise, analogous forms of barbarism. There is both melancholia and righteous anger in her final piece, 'Where Are You, Patricia Sigl?' (the name suggests signets, seals or ciphers), subtitled 'Dispatch from London, Spring 2020', but also rich limnings. Revolving – like 'Map of a Lost Soul' – around a woman who has wandered from her spot, this time a semi-destitute former Wisconsinite, it paints, in its description of a baroque Islington laced with stuffed exotic animals, side-alleys full of antiquarians, arrays of painted porcelain and fountain pens and toys and maps under 'an indented awning and a string of coloured light bulbs [that] give off the aura of an abandoned seaside pavilion' (everywhere points to somewhere else), plus, of course, bouquet-drenched funeral homes having new layers of paint applied to their exteriors, a carnival of spectres. The lead one of these, the cryptically eponymous Ms. Sigl, first glimpsed by the author in the Rare Books section of the British Library (she's an expert on the all-but-forgotten work of the eighteenth-century playwright Elizabeth Inchbald), now haunts St. Peter's and Devonia Streets, appearing hunched, cane-clasping, in the dusk – then, eventually, not appearing, leading Aridjis to wonder whether she's been relegated to a footnote in an early Inchbald edition she'll one day pick up in Camden Passage. In the Aridjis Atlas, blurred and shifting though it is, Sigl takes her place not far from those marked by the ghosts of other ageing sybils: Leonora Carrington (whom Aridjis knew intimately), Mavis Gallant, Beatrice Hastings and suchlike female troubadours. One senses that, in these figures, she finds, if not mirrors or doubles (that would be too fixed, too static), then perhaps a set of vectors – will-o'-the-wisps casting a play of light and shadow down the path of some eternal wander.

– Tom McCarthy
2021

Stories

Dialogue with
a Somnambulist

Winter has the city in its grip and at three forty-five the streetlights crackle back on, throwing a tenuous light onto everything. Lean days, little hanging to them apart from long shadows and stubborn leaves, days that become hard to measure once November arrives. Yet this has always been my favourite time of year, when a certain solitude floats through the air and from one moment to the next everything falls silent, apart from the graffiti.

I'd been at my new job for just over five months. Most afternoons ticked by without much incident and I'd watch from a distance as the other shop girls draped themselves over the sofas, the showroom their living room, trading stories at low volume. Temporary versus full time: based on this distinction and a few others, they excluded me. So I would spend my time watching the advancing clock and the immobile door or else flicking through pages of carpet samples. Our only regular client was an elderly rheumatic who would come in and try out the various armchairs and then say he'd return with his wife. No one seemed interested in what we had to offer: swivel chairs in eight colours, armchairs in three, and sofas with curves that would soothe the most troubled of souls. One night after yet another immobile day, I decided to go for a post-dinner walk. Wrapped in my woollen blue coat I ventured out into the street, the cold, the wind. It was past eleven and few people were out, and those who were disappeared into their hats and scarves, less face than accessory. I turned left and then right, weighing up the benefits of either direction. To the left lay a busy street, to the right a quieter one. A plastic bag blew past. I decided to follow it. The wind whipped it up, then sucked it back down, then buffeted it one way and another. The bag led me into the quieter street, where the only other pedestrian was a figure in a torn raincoat, one of those dark city angels who appear like holograms only to disappear a second later.

The plastic bag, insubordinate, seemed intent on resisting the fate of the other bags lining the street. The wind had dropped and yet it was unwilling to settle, now blown by a mysterious current. On and on. I followed it from one street to the next, taking routes I'd never taken. After a few minutes I grew tired of following it and decided to turn around. As I went round the last corner I bumped into the figure in the torn raincoat. One of us, or perhaps both, had been walking in circles.

Got any change, he asked in a cobwebbed voice.
No, sorry.
Well, then, can you tell me how to find Eschschloraque?

Eschschloraque may seem like a nonsense name but to some of us it stood for the finest bar in the city, one of the last survivors of bygone days. I'd read about it, heard about it, even dreamt about it, but each time I tried to go I would somehow get lost; some said that only a select few were ever able to find it, and for the rest it would remain off the map.

No, but let's look, I replied.

Before I knew it we were walking together, side by side like old friends. He seemed slightly out of breath. I slowed my steps.

After ten minutes of crossing streets and pausing on corners, we came to an alleyway. I was uncertain who had led whom: it was irrelevant. We entered the alleyway, then through one interior courtyard and another and another. Just as I was losing count, we came to a dark ramshackle building with phosphorous windows and an iron door.

This is it, said my companion, and I knew he was right.

We knocked on the door, lightly at first and then harder. Our knocks were lost in a flood of gypsy punk coming from inside. I then noticed a small buzzer to the left and pressed down. A girl with several gold teeth stuck out her head, inspected us for a few seconds, and opened the door just wide enough for us to pass. Once inside, the raincoat vanished, but I was too distracted by the décor to care where he had gone.

Everywhere I turned, I saw monsters. The smallest were crafted from papier-mâché and dangled from the ceiling like wounded birds. The medium-sized ones perched on the counters and windowsills like sullen poultry. Only the largest monsters, their crepuscular eyes fixed on the smoky darkness of the bar, were given their own showcases . . .

I knew these monsters had been made in the eighties by the Dead Chickens collective and were part of a larger monster cabinet, big mechanical grotesques with goggle eyes and amusement park tongues. I tried to imagine monster vocabulary. Big clunky words that don't fit anywhere except in the mouths of these creatures? A twilight language, used to obscure rather than illuminate? Every word uttered by one of them would steer one further and further away from meaning.

The music now playing, Einstürzende Neubauten, fit them perfectly, music like beautiful clanking, tunes that seemed to emerge from cogs and levers, pulleys and wheels. I ordered a vodka and searched for a place to sit, straining my eyes to see clearly. It felt like night, a different kind of night, had taken up residence inside. Muscly shadows drank near slim ones, lunar faces by duskier, and every now and then a streetlamp of a person, somehow more luminous than the rest, lit up the area around them.

A girl was rising from a purple sofa. I hurried over to claim it. Between the sofa and the wall, I noticed, was another showcase, though this one had a human figure inside, nothing chimerical. The figure was a good seven or eight feet tall and very slender, with jet-black hair matted to his forehead. His eyes were firmly shut and thick strokes of charcoal lined the lids and brows. His nose was straight, the entire face reigned by a quiet dignity that the monsters lacked. On the bottom was a plaque: Somnambulist.

Two evenings later, I returned to the bar. As if on autopilot, I walked down the same streets, into the same alleyway, across the same courtyards, and banged on the iron door, for the bell was now missing. The same girl with gold teeth opened it. It was Wednesday eve, and the place was emptier, with only a few lone customers here and there. Drink, sofa, somnambulist.

Tall and regal and encased in darkness, his eyes and lips remained shut while the sharp diagonals of his cheekbones divided his face into planes. This time, I inspected him from top to bottom. Black turtleneck, black leggings, hips narrower than shoulders. With his large, square-toed shoes, he looked like a dormant mime. After two drinks by his side, I stood up and left, casting one final unreciprocated glance as I walked away.

It did not take long for Eschschloraque to become my second home. I would visit three times a week, sometimes four. Sometimes directly after work, often later. The clientele tended to vary, particularly in its male-to-female ratio, and I had yet to exchange a word with anyone. The girl with the gold teeth was always there, and though we'd never spoken she knew my drink and would reach for the Absolut as soon as I approached the counter.

Listless faces and still hands, minds that drifted far from the present. Empty glasses outnumbered filled ones, and few people ordered seconds. Everyone was in exile from something or someone, it seemed. As for the monsters dangling from the ceiling, perched on the counters or imprisoned in the showcases, after a while their novelty wore off and I hardly stopped to look.

Yet the somnambulist still held sway. The glass pane of his vitrine was getting clouded; I hoped someone would clean it soon.

One night as I sat staring into the showcase, I felt a tap on my shoulder. It was Friedrich, a former boyfriend. He fetched a drink and came to sit by my side. His face was round, had lost definition, and his eyes had grown pouchy, but I could see the old him peering out from beneath. He rolled a cigarette and told me about his latest exploits – new ways to stay afloat, schemes that required a burst of energy rather than sustained endeavour – and I told him about the furniture shop. We wondered together whether either of us would ever be able to take on something more permanent.

The bargirl put on Gogol Bordello and dragged the tables to the sides of the room, opening up a space at the centre. The monsters in the showcases seemed to lollop to the music, and once I put down my glass Friedrich grabbed my hand and pulled me into the crowd to dance. I did my best to keep up, always with my back to the showcase, with the sense, for the first time, I was being watched.

The weeks passed. Sales: four armchairs, three tables, two carpets and a teak dresser that was returned a day later.

One Sunday afternoon Friedrich rang and insisted I go over. After putting on the kettle he said he had something to show me, but only once the tea was ready. The kettle took its time but finally whistled. Mugs in hand, I followed him from the kitchen to his bedroom. The space, lined by vinyl and paperbacks, brought back a rush of memories. He motioned to his wardrobe and told me to open it. I walked over and pulled on one of the knobs. The door stuck and I had to tug harder. The second time, it gave, and I nearly fell backwards when I saw what was inside.

There he stood, tall and erect, hair matted and face serene. I studied the mould of his closed lids, the way the bottom line of his eyes echoed the brows, the gentle mouth. He was without a doubt a work of art, and now that the glass was gone I could admire the wax skin, which glowed in the darkening room.

Friedrich could tell I was in need of an explanation. So he explained. He said he'd got him for me, could tell I had a bit of a predilection. He got him for me, he repeated, for a small fee. And who ever heard of shutting up a somnambulist when movement was what defined them. So there it was. He only wanted three hundred.

I stared at the wax figure and placed my right hand on his chest. No heartbeat. I stood on tiptoe and touched his cheek, smooth and cool, then dropped my hand to feel the pulseless throat that rose like a tower from his turtleneck.

Friedrich watched me watch him. I asked whether this was stolen loot. No, he answered, he'd come to an agreement with the girl with the gold teeth; they'd agreed he'd be happier at my place.

I thought about it for two minutes, all sorts of thoughts rushing this way and that in my head, and said yes. We shook on it and then toasted with our mugs of tea.

That night we waited till Friedrich's neighbours had all gone quiet and then wrapped the wax man in a dark sheet, king size because of his height. We tilted him sideways and carried him out of the flat, down the stairs and into the street. He weighed much less than I'd been expecting; I hadn't realised the wax was hollow. Into Friedrich's estate car and a ten-minute drive to my flat, where I frantically searched for keys while Friedrich complained about the awkward shape of our burden. He'd been carrying the feet, and the large square shoes refused to come off.

We decided on a corner of my bedroom that couldn't be seen from the window. Impatient to inspect the features up close, I shone a halogen lamp onto his face and stepped back. Just as I was beginning to re-admire all the features, Friedrich came running up and redirected the lamp towards the ceiling. Never do that, he said.

My first night alone with the somnambulist. I sat up in bed, drew my covers around me and stared timidly across the room. It was easier when there was a pane of glass between us. The hours passed. Nothing. I began to wonder whether Friedrich was being fanciful when he said the wax figure would be happier with me.

In any event, if he was to live in my home he had to have a name. The next morning before going to work I skimmed the titles on my bookshelf. I didn't want something too common but I didn't want something too farfetched, so I looked towards the history books, past the poetry and prose. Cristobal or Maximilian – no. Tarquin, Merlin or Percival – definitely not. Finally my eyes settled on *Italian Art through the Ages*. I opened it to a random page about the mighty Vesuvius. From that moment onwards, he would be called Pompeii.

When Friedrich visited the furniture shop that afternoon my colleagues swivelled their heads in hunger and curiosity. What news, he asked, to which I replied, None. Just wait another day or two.

Two nights later I was reading in bed when a new sound entered the room. I laid down my book and listened. A light breathing. Was I imagining it? The eyes started to open. The lids trembled, the lids lifted halfway, and then, all of a sudden, they sprang open to reveal pitch-black pupils, and in one quick second I was taken in.

Up rose an arm, stiffly at first and then more assertively. And then the other. After this initial stretch, his arms dropped and the legs began, two long spindly legs that had forgotten how to walk. The somnambulist tested each one out several times before taking his first step forwards.

I followed him quietly as he left the room and went down the corridor. Twice he stopped as if to change direction but continued. Once in the living room, he headed for a pair of boots I'd left by the sofa. The boots were soiled, the residue of a rainy day, and patches of dirt rubbed off on his turtleneck as he carried them to my bedroom and dropped them with a thud in the closet.

Finished with the task, Pompeii turned back to me. His gaze was glassy and hard to read. Soon he was standing three centimetres away, then two and then one, all kinds of distances quickly bridged as he bent down to kiss my mouth. It was a dry kiss but one given with force, and his lips remained pressed against my own for several seconds. I was too astonished to kiss back but remembered to close my eyes. Kiss delivered, he returned to his corner and went still.

The following night I sat in bed and waited for him to move. At midnight the eyes opened and the lips began to part but the sound that came out seemed to emerge from a metal box with ancient hinges. After the same brief stretch he walked out of the bedroom and down the corridor, this time pacing the length of it rather than going on to the living room. Every now and then he'd pause outside a door as if to pursue a new thought, then resume his pacing till he returned to stillness.

The next day as I rested my head against his chest, I noticed a dank smell. It occurred to me he'd probably never been bathed. I couldn't submerge him in water but there were other ways of improving his hygiene, so while he slept I combed his synthetic hair and ran a damp towel over the exposed parts of his body. After a few rubs the odour was replaced by the scent of honey.

The next time he started to move, Pompeii headed straight for a crumpled envelope on the windowsill and a pen stuck in the grooves of a radiator, as if having decided while still inactive what his focus would be. I had tidied up and felt there was nothing left to find but he quickly discovered the two items I'd overlooked. Once the pen and envelope had been deposited in a drawer, he refolded a shelf of sweaters in my room. The objects of his choice would vary, yet shoes were a big attraction, followed by books and records.

One night as I heated some soup in the kitchen, Pompeii walked in. He took one look at the flames licking the sides of the pan and went tense and treelike. By the time I lowered the heat he was gone. Out of respect I have quit smoking and the one box of matches I kept now lives in a drawer. Whether he feels any relation to candles is a mystery, but I've put them away too just in case.

Friedrich dropped by to check in. How's our somnambulist, he asked, to which I replied, Come see for yourself. After inspecting him we went to the kitchen and he taught me a new card game. The hours went by. We ordered food, opened a bottle of wine, played another game, opened another bottle. As we were reshuffling the deck there was a noise at the door. There he stood, tall and regal, looking straight at us. I waved but he didn't react. And when Friedrich started to greet him he turned around and headed back to my room, where he went still for the rest of the night.

The obsession with tidying has begun to lose its charm. Especially now that Pompeii has started hiding things rather than putting them away. I often have trouble finding my shoes and have been late to work more than once. Most nights Friedrich and I stay up playing cards, and whenever he is over Pompeii refuses to shift from his spot.

One Friday evening, seized by an impulse to change setting, we went for a walk through Kreuzberg and ended up at the Goldene Hahn, one of our old haunts. As we sat there over wine and a few small dishes, all I could think about was Pompeii. But the image of him awakened guilt rather than desire. Was he up, and if so, what would he be doing in the flat without me? The usual activities or something new? As we left the restaurant Friedrich slipped his arm around my waist. He gripped me tightly and soon we were in his flat, in his bed, and the sensation of soft, warm skin was like kerosene.

The next morning when I came home the smell of honey was overwhelming. I ran from room to room. Nothing in the kitchen, nothing in the living room. The corridor and bathroom, fine too. The smell was coming from elsewhere. I rushed to my bedroom. A light was seeping from under the door, though I hadn't left any lights on the day before. Inside, I discovered the halogen lamp shining directly onto Pompeii. His features had started to blur, a small stream of wax dribbled from his chin, tracing a line down his body and hardening into a small pool on the floor. More wax from his fingertips. I ran over to turn off the lamp.

After a few hours, Pompeii's body recovered its rigidity. The danger had passed. I stood back and studied the face, the hair, the once delicate chin and fingers that I'd had to remould. He was still handsome, but not quite as handsome as before.

That night, and the following and the following, Pompeii remained fixed to his spot, eyes closed and arms straight as lances. I kissed his mouth, kissed his neck and his hands, and for the first time ever I felt I was kissing a candle. Each night I'd sit and wait for movement, for the large eyes to spring open and the head to swivel in my direction. I left things out, but they were no longer picked up. My flat became messier by the day. Poking the hard stomach, Friedrich would comment on the chaos.

Following a lengthy discussion, we decided to donate Pompeii to the city's wax museum. It was a large, lively place, apparently, visited by people of all ages. Once the decision had been made there seemed little sense in waiting, so the next morning we wrapped him up and drove over.

As Friedrich negotiated the traffic, taking a longer route than necessary, I lifted the sheet and regarded, again with more guilt than desire, the mass of wax that had shared my home for four months.

The museum was housed in a mansion of red brick, its entrance guarded by a startlingly realistic Golem with a helmet of hair. The interior had dark wooden floors and thick red carpets, with a large iron staircase winding up to the second floor.

What splendid artistry, the manager exclaimed when we stripped off the sheet to reveal the figure beneath. What a beautifully painted face, what a graciously formed body.

A pang – were we giving away a great work of art?

She thanked us again for the donation and offered me a free pass to use as often as I liked.

Where would they put him, I asked.

Up on the second floor, with the other film stars.

Film stars?

Why yes, she said, wasn't he the somnambulist from the Caligari film?

I wasn't sure what she was talking about but noticed Friedrich nodding with a smile. We all shook hands. The deal was done. And yet it hadn't quite been a deal, for I was leaving empty-handed, a feeling that only deepened once I got home. But I also felt unencumbered, I had to admit, and that was something to bear in mind.

After a week had elapsed I left work early one afternoon and went to visit Pompeii. When I presented my pass the receptionist mentioned I was only the third visitor that day. And yet it was nearly four thirty.

I remarked that I'd thought the museum was popular, especially with children.

No longer, she said. The city now has many more exciting attractions.

I proceeded directly to the second floor. The first room I entered was full of stiff dignitaries from around the world, religious and political figures from Russia, India, Germany and elsewhere. Along with the same sombre stance, I noticed they all had glass eyes, an immediate giveaway: too much shine. That was one of the things, I realised, which distinguished Pompeii from the other wax folk.

Higher-voltage lighting announced the film star section. Richard Burton and Elizabeth Taylor, Marilyn Monroe, Marlon Brando and James Dean. The Peter Lorre figure was especially captivating, lurking a few steps away from Marlene Dietrich at her piano, a half-smoked cigarette balanced between two keys. And then, towards the back of the room, I spotted a tall figure in black. His eyes were closed, his chin still slightly uneven, yet he had the same elegance and dignity that'd struck me at the bar with the iron door. I rushed to his side and stroked his arm for forgiveness. But I was met with silence of all sorts. I'll visit often, I promised, aware that it was little consolation.

Two months went by. Each week I'd visit the film star section and speak to him, relaying details of my life without ever mentioning Friedrich. Pompeii had yet to acknowledge my presence.

Summer sales arrived and everything at the shop bore a big red label, each piece of furniture just waiting to become part of a home and acquire some history. It'd been five weeks since I'd gone to see Pompeii. Friedrich and I were still spending nights together but nothing had been finalised.

On my next visit to the museum I forgot to bring my pass but the receptionist recognised me and let me through. Impatient to see my wax man again, I climbed the stairs two at a time. But when I arrived at the film stars, Pompeii was no longer there behind Peter Lorre and company. I rushed back down to the receptionist.

Is something the matter? she asked, seeing me breathless. Where is the somnambulist?

He's been moved downstairs, down to the basement with the other ghouls.

I nearly tripped down the stairs to the basement, dreading what I would find. As I descended, the light dimmed and a musty smell thickened the air. The first exhibit to greet me was the Bleeding Nun, a woman in a floor-length habit stained with blood. A rosary dangled from her waist and most of her face was covered by a veil, leaving only the outline of a wailing mouth. In one hand a lantern, in the other a dagger. A cackle away was Frankenstein's monster, rising from the table where he was created. And then Doctor Frankenstein himself with a mad leer. Two schoolchildren, the only other humans around, were daring one another to touch the bolts on the monster's neck.

The torture chamber was next, where an elfin creature chained to a post lifted its head every few seconds and clanked its chain. Nearby were two more homely individuals, one strapped to a wooden wheel and the other to a protean table. Every few seconds one of them would let out a ghastly bellow.

In the next room, lit by the glimmer of a plastic-flamed candelabrum, I found him. There was my somnambulist, now labelled a monster, flanked by Dracula and the Wolfman. A bluish tinge crept over his face, his eyes were tightly shut. As I stroked his arm, neck and lips I sensed his retreat was deeper than ever.

That night I told Friedrich I wanted to sleep alone. As I lay in bed staring at the corner where Pompeii used to be, I thought of him stuck in that dungeon of strangled howls. And I then thought of him in his first home, and how those monsters had at least left him in peace. I finally managed to close my eyes, but all I could see were nuns dancing on the lids.

Saturday afternoon I was in the midst of rearranging my record collection when the phone rang. It was the manager of the wax museum. There'd been a fire. The police had yet to discover the cause – short circuit or arson – but the fact was, the entire collection had been lost.

Friedrich met me there. The disaster site had already become a local spectacle, with legions of onlookers crowding round the building, pointing and shouting as they tried to size up the damage. The facade was deeply charred, the roof had caved in, and the windows were two hollowed eyes gaping back at us. A group of policemen stood near the entrance, by what remained of the Golem, a collapsed mass and a helmet of hair. We showed them our pass and went in. Inside, every direction seemed to be cordoned off. The smell of burnt wax was overpowering.

In the main hall lay dozens of outfits and accessories

trapped in the hardened wax of their former owners. Period shoes and historical costumes, a plumed headdress and a crumpled cape: the sad remains of the stately figures that had for decades held court in the museum. Faces melted into puddles, bodies into pools, different locks of hair all clumped together. Once a spectrum of distinct colours, the wax was now a confusion of black and green and red and purple.

From between a pair of lace boots a dissolved face peered up at me, its rouged cheeks and fake pearl necklace still intact.

On my way to the horror section a guard informed me that the lights had been turned off to prevent further short circuits. Friedrich lent me his lighter and I crossed the red tape and started down the spiral staircase, the burnt wax ever more potent. The first remains I came across were those of the Bleeding Nun, reduced to a singed habit and a creamy puddle, the beads from her rosary scattered across the floor. In the torture chamber, the victims had melted into or onto their instruments of torture, trapped between spokes or hardened onto tables.

In the next room I searched desperately for familiar features, the black eyes, the straight nose, the fine lips. After stepping around various zones of wax I came to an area of marbled grey, the product, I assumed, of charcoal and white. My fears were confirmed by the dark tufts of hair freed from the forehead they'd once framed. A few feet away, in a pile, were the black turtleneck, leggings and shoes. The museum guard shrugged when I said I wanted to collect what was left and didn't think there'd be a problem. But we had to wait for confirmation from the manager, who was currently in a press conference.

Someone emerged from a room and tacked the press release to a bulletin board in the main entrance:

The fire at the wax museum started at approximately 2:37 this morning and lasted for over three hours. It is now thought to be the result of faulty wiring. The wooden floors and carpets contributed to the rapid spread of the flames, which consumed all 250 figures in the collection. The four truckfuls of firemen who arrived at the site at 3:15 were unable to extinguish the fire. The museum is the property of the von Pezold family, who visited the site this morning. Ludwig von Pezold, the owner's son, lamented the loss of the wax figures, whose value is estimated at between 10,000 and 30,000 euros. Some of the figures will be impossible to replace, such as the figure of John Paul II, personally blessed by the pope himself during his visit to the city. The von Pezold family reckons it will take approximately two years to rebuild the collection.

A guard sent me to wait in a hall that until two days ago served as the Room of the Revolution, where figures towered in proud, upright poses over citizens who came to stare at their swords, rifles and camouflage, dreaming of lives they themselves would never have the courage to lead. To one side of what was once Che Guevara, a pool of wax beside a sparse moustache and beret, I found a bench and sat down to survey the destruction, trying to imagine the sorts of figures that had been. A rumpled green cloak, a camouflage shirt, a pair of combat boots. Yet what I'd failed to notice earlier were the dozens of large marbles and hundreds of small square white chips lying about, many of them embedded in the wax. I picked up a marble and turned it around: it was a medical glass eye, a perfect sphere with a delicately painted blue pupil with thin red veins radiating from its centre. The small square chips, I realised, were of smooth porcelain. These wax figures had porcelain teeth. And what about my Pompeii? I never saw the inside of his mouth.

Friedrich appeared. He'd spoken to the manager, who said it was fine for us to remove what was left of our friend.

It took four hours to scrape Pompeii off the museum floor with blunt knives lent to us by a guard. The wax was stubborn and we had to tackle it from different angles. Friedrich found a plastic bag into which we threw all the chunks. Everything smelled of honey. We decided to leave the clothes since they were burnt and bedraggled and adhered to the wax of others. I never found the large, dark eyes.

When we finished gathering the remains, Friedrich asked if he could keep the shoes. Yes, I said. He removed his boots and slipped them on. The fit was perfect, we had to agree, as he paraded around the room.

Faits Divers

After two lion cubs and three rattlesnakes were reported missing, investigators discovered that the zoo director, Charles Hunt, 58, was also a dealer in wild animal skins.

Uncertain which street to take, György Szerb, the distinguished Hungarian cartographer in town for a wedding, stepped into traffic and was instantly struck.

After decades of hearing his own voice, recorded in 1997 in a studio in Hammersmith, announcing the stations, Herbert Stift, 48, leapt in front of an oncoming train.

Shuffling through Hampton Court in felt slippers to protect the floors, Anthony Lang, 69, suffered a heart attack and was unable to finish the tour.

In a small coastal town, the thieves' main focus was an old cash register rather than the awkward silence of the pet store at night.

It wasn't until the fifth turn of the carousel that the horse came flying off; horse and screw have been reinstated, the boy, 7-year-old Timothy Clay of Croydon, remains in hospital.

Forty-six hipsters, seven academics and one vagabond gathered in London Fields to hear the cultural theorist from New York.

After seeing their designs directly copied, Hamburg Dioramas Ltd. have decided to take their British rivals, Humbug Dioramas Ltd., to court.

The bodies of Lucy Stout and Nick Ackles, a young couple from Leytonstone, were found in the canal only this week; she suffered from melancholia, he from a rare blood disease.

In the town of Prickwillow, near Ely, an entire family – husband, wife and child – have been shot by their 24-year-old lodger. He had published two poems in the local paper; they trusted him.

A kitchen extension, four new bookcases and a large conservatory: once the work was complete, Lady Carol Jenks, 75, knifed her husband in the neck and ran off with one of the builders.

After building a five-turreted castle and laying all seven of his silver rings on the sand, the divorced bassist waded into the sea at Brighton and never came out.

Doctors are trying to establish whether Akko Markku of Helsinki, 51, who attended the annual Lightning Survivor

Conference in London, died of an aneurysm or severe dehydration.

After threatening suicide for weeks, Mrs. Hart of Seven Sisters ate herself to death; six years ago, her husband, John, died during an electrical storm.

An aggressive form of curlicued purple vegetation, neighbours say, was responsible for the suffocation of two retired historians in North Kensington.

It is thought the murdered prostitute came from Germany; in her bag, they discovered a saxophone-shaped biscuit, two sets of maroon shoelaces and a book by Brecht.

Due to grain mutations in southern France, six people in central London developed week-long headaches and three began speaking in code.

An eight-foot bird with red eyes has been spotted circling over south-west London; planes at Heathrow have been diverted.

Pigeon

She tried to straighten her thoughts, give them some order and linearity, and when that didn't work she imagined herself elsewhere, on a mountain or coast far from the city, rather than on the Central Line with its erratic movement and office-bound passengers and the prickly silence of those torn from sleep. She and her mother had been lucky to find seats; at that hour the Tube was nearly full, a geometric overload of skirts and suits, and wherever she turned she saw freshly combed hair and painted faces, newspapers, briefcases all vying for space.

'You know, you could have died.' Her mother lowered her voice in the hope that none of the other passengers would hear.
'Well, the point is, I didn't.'
'You nearly did.'
'I'm cold.'
'Don't you have a sweater in your bag?'
'I gave it away.'
'You gave it away?'
'This morning. To one of the nurses.'

With something close to nostalgia, N. thought back on the small room she'd just left behind, its itchy grey blanket and sweat-faded sheets, and the dent in the wall, courtesy of a former patient, in which her own fist had fit perfectly. Now that she'd left, she found herself missing the kind female voices that roused her each morning, voices that for a few seconds invoked the promise of a new life, voices she preferred to that of her mother. And she thought back too on the strange dreams she'd had, dangerous and ornate, dreams unlike the ones outside. And then the wallpaper: red and white stripes connecting floor to ceiling, heaven to hell. There was a window, always locked, but as a view N. preferred the walls and the ceiling since they didn't present any mocking beyond.

In the seat in front of her sat a boy wearing headphones. She hadn't heard any music in five weeks, she realised, not a note. As soon as she got home she would listen to . . . everything. Thousands and thousands of songs. She'd go through them all, one by one, day and night, an endless carousel, memories welcome and unwelcome, a melodic loop of acceptances and rejections, tiny triumphs and huge disasters. In the clinic, what she'd most feared was the loss of her memories; now she was willing to keep them all.

'Which sweater was it?'
'Hmm?'
'Which sweater?'
'Just a sweater.'
'I hope not one of the ones I bought you last month.'
She shrugged.

'They won't be on sale again. You won't have one like that again.' She shrugged a second time.

'She must have been a very nice nurse to deserve a sweater like that.'

'Yes, she was nice and kind and brought me tea whenever I wanted.'

'Shouldn't they do that anyway?'

'Well, they don't.'

Her mother shook her head and mumbled something to herself, as if running a few mental sums, trying to assess whether she had possibly, in this latest guilt venture, been taken for a ride.

N. looked down at her hands, which had nearly recovered their delicate form. There'd been a point when she hadn't recognised them, they were so purple and swollen she feared they would break off and drift away, the palms puffy and indistinct, a fortune-teller's nightmare. And then she wondered, as she rubbed them together, what had happened to her gloves, a beautiful pair her grandmother once knitted, dark blue with grey borders. They'd begun to feel tight so she'd stowed them away, but where? Well, it didn't matter, what was gone was gone. Just as long as no one touched her records, the only belongings N. swore to herself she would never sell. This past year everything, pretty much everything, had gone up in smoke, part of an amazing alchemical transformation of base metal into gold.

She couldn't help but keep an eye on the doors. Instinct. Each time they opened and closed at a station, an opportunity came and went.

At the next stop, two men clutching paper bags from McDonald's got on. The carriage filled up with the tantalising smell of french fries.

'I'm cold and I'm hungry.'

'I'll make you something when we get home.'

'That's ages away.'

Her mother looked up at the map on the wall. 'Only twelve more stops.'

'And then the bus.'

'There shouldn't be traffic at this hour.'

'I don't see why we couldn't take a cab.'

'A cab would've cost the same as a day at the clinic.'

'Then think of all the money I'm saving you by leaving now.'

'I just hope Dr. Reid knew what he was talking about when he said you were ready to come home.'

Coming home: once upon a time, quite a while ago now, this phrase was like a magic potion, but the word 'home' had now been attached to so many spaces, it'd lost all currency. Each year it had referred to somewhere else, to a different scenario, a different roof, a different set of faces: the rented flat in Bow, the rented flat in Seven Sisters, the family house in Mexico before her mother went off with the Englishman, and of course the string of clinics where she'd been sent after the first so-called intervention.

At Oxford Circus half the carriage disembarked, leaving room for the dozens of passengers who clambered on. Nearly everyone found a seat and those who didn't grabbed on to the bright red poles and handrails as the Tube began to pull out of the station. N. rubbed her arm and thought back on the handsome new patient who'd arrived at the clinic two days earlier. She could still visualise him perfectly, ambling down the corridor with his combed-back hair and long-sleeved turtleneck, no track marks visible, only the familiar scent of melancholy. It was his fourth time there, the nurses said, and they doubted it would be the last. He'd looked over in her direction once or twice, at least she thought he had . . . If her mother hadn't arrived so early that morning they might have spoken.

'Twitch, twitch, twitch,' her mother interrupted the reverie. 'Twitch twitch twitch. I thought they'd ironed all the twitches out of you.'

'I set some aside for the journey home.'

Yes, her mother had tried. But only for a few months and not hard enough. Her attempts were half-hearted, mechanical, and she'd been careless – forgetting to dispose of expired medication, leaving earrings and banknotes within view, passing on phone calls that should have been screened: endless temptations for the easily tempted. She hadn't tried as hard as some of the other mothers, at least according to the stories people shared, and she certainly hadn't been very present in the early days, when N. had desperately needed her.

It was at Chancery Lane that the pigeon flew in, right into the carriage in a clean diagonal sweep, a whisk of all four seasons compressed into one. It was a large pigeon, slate grey with reddish eyes and white-tipped wings, and it entered at the last possible second before the doors banged shut and the Tube recommenced its journey.

One moment it had been on a vaulted platform with friends, the next, it found itself alone with *the other species* inside a closed space in motion. Almost immediately, with the first awkward movements of the train, the bird turned into a dervish of feathers, panic and confusion. People ducked and dispersed yet it still managed to graze a few heads and shoulders. Two startled young women rose from their seats and hurried to the opposite end of the carriage. Someone waved a handbag.

The pigeon flapped this way and that and N. caught a glimpse of its underwing, of an inverse serenity, light powdery grey. Each stroke of its wings released a slight breeze, the breeze of hundreds of flights across the city.

'Ssssss,' someone hissed when the bird came too near.

After about a minute or two of useless histrionics, the pigeon seemed to calm down and landed on the floor with a thick, clumsy thud. It surveyed the area and then headed enthusiastically in the direction of the men with bags from McDonald's. One of them stamped his boot and muttered something in a foreign language. The pigeon backed off.

N. and her mother watched on. The other passengers watched too. No one spoke, no one moved. All eyes were on the bird.

At St. Paul's, a station N. rarely used, a woman with a dark ponytail got on and took an empty seat near them, straightening out her skirt as she sat down. The woman pulled a novel out of her bag, cracked the spine wide open and turned to the first page. When the pigeon pecked at something near her feet, she simply moved them a few inches to the left without looking up from her book.

When had she last read? N. couldn't remember. She'd started countless books, of that she was sure, novels and biographies and even some poetry. But despite the warm glow that rose from the pages she would doze off before long and find herself, hours later, with the book in her lap or at her feet, and she'd put it aside and pick up the next one, and this too, she realised, was an endless carousel, though instead of a whole variety of memories the main memory the books summoned was of herself as a university student before she dropped out, and of her prodigious concentration, remarked on by everyone, and her proud rows of 10s.

Swoosh, swoosh. The pigeon was back in the air and had begun flapping more frantically than ever. It circled a pole, zipped down the carriage, zipped back near where N. and her mother were sitting. People would hastily make way for it, clearing a path for its desperation, but it didn't want to *see*. At one point mid-tunnel it flew into a darkened window and was thrown to the floor for a few seconds before resuming its flight.

At the next station N. grabbed a sports section that had been left behind and tried to usher the bird out, but it grew even more flustered and headed in the opposite direction just as the doors were closing.

'He prefers it in here, where it's warm,' someone said. No one laughed.

At Liverpool Street a serious-looking man in a pinstriped suit strode on and sat directly across from them, the aroma of McDonald's replaced by the confident reign of cologne. The man was hefty, with cheeks bearing the flush of countryside and pale blue eyes that with one glance sized up the other passengers. He set down his briefcase, wedging it between his polished black shoes, and unfolded the newspaper he had under his arm. Soon all N. could see were shoes, large knuckles and knees and the outspread wings of *The Telegraph*.

'By the way,' her mother turned to her, 'we've decided you're going to Mexico for a year.'

For the first time since her last fix, she was aware of the blood circulating through her body.

'A year?'

'You're going to live with your father. We've discussed it and agree it's the best option.'

'I'm happy here.'

'You know you're not. This is your last chance.'

There'd been many last chances; she was nearing the end of her supply.

'What will I do there?'

'You'll live with your father and start thinking a little more seriously about the future.'

'Of course, the future . . .'

Little by little, it had come to represent nothing more than a shadowy road lit by fireflies, lined on either side by the silhouettes of people and possibilities that would remain just that, silhouettes.

The woman reading the novel let out a small cry. The pigeon had flown past a little too close, brushing her cheek. In a delayed response she waved a hand in front of her face and leaned back as far as she could but there was no need, it had already flapped away. A grey feather zigzagged to the floor.

'Three more stops,' said N.'s mother.

It was shortly after she said this, N. would never forget, that the pigeon flew right into the centre of *The Telegraph*. Without blinking, the man in the pinstriped suit laid down his paper and within what seemed like a fraction of a second, grabbed the bird – the whole carriage was now watching – and with his fat knuckles snapped its neck. It was a clean snap, expertly done, as if he'd been snapping birds' necks his entire life.

One second the pigeon had been tense and aquiver, the next it was an immobile lump of grey. Whatever its journey across the city had been, it ended here. The man deposited the corpse on the empty seat next to him, picked up his paper and continued to read.

The act was met with silence. Everyone simply stared at the dead bird, just stared and stared, as if pooled together the intensity of their gaze might resurrect it.

For a few seconds N. fought the impulse to pick up the pigeon and take it outside to bury – the sanitation people would surely just toss it in a bin – but the thought of touching the thing made her queasy. She imagined what it would feel like to hold the feathery corpse, still warmed by its recent life force, and wasn't sure what was more overpowering, her distress at witnessing such brutality or the guilty flicker of revulsion she'd begun to feel.

As if in quiet defeat, the pigeon's head lay to one side like the emblem on a fallen coat of arms. Its eye had almost immediately turned white, or perhaps it was the eyelid that had closed, and its legs, already stiff, looked like little pink twigs that could easily break off.

N. turned to look at her mother, who continued staring at the bird, willing her to say something, anything. But no, she kept whatever she was thinking to herself, hands in lap, fingers interlocked.

At the following station, which was open air, the business-man folded his paper, picked up his briefcase and stepped out. The doors of the Tube took a few moments to close, and as they stuttered shut N. gazed out at the sky and the platform and the spaces in between, seized by the urge to grab her bag and run for it, in whatever direction opened up to her. But she remained in her seat and with one strong tug unzipped her jacket, for the temperature inside the carriage suddenly felt very warm.

A Celebration of the Circus Flea

There are no limits to wonderment when it comes to this pocket-sized performer, cruelly underrated within the animal kingdom and treated even more poorly by humans. In reality, the flea yearns for attention and is eager to please, which makes it an ideal creature to train for the circus.

Fleas have strong familial bonds and it is therefore advisable to work with a family rather than with a group of random fleas. Family members know each other's antics and can easily improvise to ensure that each act runs smoothly. Grandfather fleas tend to be sensitive about retirement; it is important to include them in main tent events and mention them in any publicity.

The first step is, of course, to establish a relationship of trust between yourself and the flea. Let it know that you do not plan to squash it between your fingers, even if it does bite you once or twice. It is worth mentioning that fleas are curious beings and need to know what each new friend tastes like. A small nip is all you will feel, followed by a subsequent itch that should not last longer than twenty-four hours. If your flea is overly curious, there is a eucalyptus lotion you can rub on your hands, feet and neck. The danger of this deterrent, however, is that your flea will avoid you altogether, and thus bring the training to an abrupt end. Generations of flea wranglers have accepted that at any given moment there will be at least one part of their body that itches; this is a minor setback of the profession.

Once you have ingratiated yourself with your star performer and its family, the stage is set to begin . . . Fleas, like other circus animals, expect to be rewarded with treats after every brave performance. Therefore you may find yourself offering your thumb each time your flea does as it's told. This is cheaper than providing other people's thumbs. The occasional use of a small tuning fork is also advised in order to prod along your performers, whose attention span ranges from the highly motivated to the sloppy and inert. There is no telling how a flea will react when given orders; even the sweetest temperament can turn sour if its pride is put on the line.

Which brings me to the next point. It is best to avoid the wrath of the circus flea. Ordinary fleas have less insight into the human psyche but performing fleas that have trained with us have a sharper notion of how to make our species suffer. What can one measly flea do to me, you may ask . . . Well, one flea may not accomplish a great deal, but there exists a vast, unspoken solidarity between fleas, and your adversary will in no time summon a tiny yet powerful army whose only aim is to make you suffer. And suffer you will, from the moment you slip your arm through that sleeve or your legs through those trousers or realise, as you read in bed, that the dots of ink on the page are alive.

With regard to safety, fleas delight in taking chances. Tightrope walkers and trapeze artists generally work without a net and get into a huff should you but suggest one. They like to think of their bodies as flexible and unbreakable. If a flea falls off the tightrope, it will almost certainly bounce back up again. Even our clairvoyant flea, whose tiny cloth turban weighs down its head, plays with its life each time it negotiates the rim of a cup filled with hot Turkish coffee.

Fearless and determined, the circus flea moves through life with great freedom, elasticity and resilience. The palm of a hand, the surface of a table, an upturned shoebox: give it a few minutes and it will create its own stage. Word has it that the grandfather fleas are in the process of setting up their own academy; soon, no one will have any need for our guidance.

The Kafka Society

It was a busy day at the headquarters of the Franz Kafka Society. Typewriters clicked away, filling the air with atonal music. A few members in the main office hummed while they prepared the events of the following year: an international congress in Prague, pilgrimages to Kafka sites in the city and beyond, the annual meeting and, finally, the endless encounters between the Society's non-academic members, who felt as passionately as those who'd written tomes on his work. One had to include everyone, give every member a sense of importance. Whether someone had formally analysed a story or novel was irrelevant – the only requirement was unconditional admiration. Most members placed Kafka above all other writers in their own national canons, quoted Kafka in most conversations and had predominantly Kafka books on their bookshelves. That wasn't too much to ask from a member of the Society.

An irascible mood gripped Mrs. Lanska that morning. Not only had membership dropped by over one hundred in the past year, but the most recent newsletter had been set in the worst type imaginable. No one would be able to read the minuscule script, save with the help of a magnifying glass. She turned the page over and over in her hands, reading it from different angles. This time the layout assistant had erred in a serious way.

The annual meeting was only a few weeks away and there were still scores of details to settle. Mrs. Lanska realised she had not read a word of Kafka in weeks, so busy had she been as President of the Society.

There came a timid knock on her office door, followed by the postman. 'Here is your mail for today, Mrs. Lanska,' he said softly, setting down a thick pile of letters. Before she had time to thank him, he had slipped out of the room and gently closed the door. If only everyone were so discreet. She glanced at the pile on the corner of her desk and readjusted her glasses. More mail than usual had arrived, although half the letters were probably bills rather than gushing letters about Kafka. One could usually tell by the address on the envelope: personal letters by hand, bureaucratic matters by machine.

Bills, receipts, a few queries, several proposals for future meetings and events, and then one letter which made her pause. Written across a striking cornflower-blue envelope was the most beautiful handwriting she had ever seen. Flourishes in abundance, perfectly straight lines, margins respected. She held up the one-page letter and read:

> Please may I join your Society. I am sixteen years old and have no friends, but I love Kafka. My parents don't give me an allowance so I can't pay your fees, but I love Kafka. Please may I belong.
>
> 'Whoever leads a solitary life and yet now and then wants to attach himself somewhere . . . he

will not be able to manage for long without a window looking on to the street.'

Yours truly, Maurice G.

Touched, Mrs. Lanska read the letter several times before pulling out a sheet of her stationery and responding:

Dear Maurice,

I do not usually grant exceptions to our membership rules but was moved by your letter. If you write and tell me your favourite Kafka stories, I will let you join the Franz Kafka Society at no cost. I hope to hear from you shortly.

Kind regards, Mrs. L

Three days later, another cornflower-blue envelope arrived. Mrs. Lanska plucked it from the pile and tore it open. Written in grand flourishes:

Dear Mrs. L,

I would like to extend my deepest gratitude for allowing me to join the Society. Few moments in my life have offered me such pleasure as when I read your letter inviting me to join. The moment I read the news I ran upstairs to show my mother, who loves Kafka too but prefers Robert Walser. In answer to your query, my favourite Kafka stories, in order of preference, are:

1. 'A Report to an Academy' (I like all stories that feature animals)
2. 'Investigations of a Dog'
3. 'The Judgment' (though I can't bear the ending)
4. 'A Hunger Artist'

Should I go on? I could list every single one of Kafka's stories in order of preference, but fear I may bore you.

Yours truly, Maurice G.

Mrs. Lanska again felt the urge to reply immediately. When her assistant entered her office to inquire about lunch she bid her to never interrupt again unless it was something of the utmost importance, for she foresaw a heavy workload over the next few months.

And thus an intense and almost daily correspondence arose between the President of the Kafka Society and the young man named Maurice. Each day when the mail was brought, Mrs. Lanska would zip through until she found the cornflower-blue envelope. On days when there wasn't an envelope of that colour, she would snap at everyone and go home early.

In accompaniment to her letters, which became longer and more detailed, she made sure to send Maurice the Society newsletter and updates on all the events. She even parted with a limited edition of Kafka stories of which she held two copies.

Maurice's letters were intimate yet equally distant; they related countless moments of his daily life, but often through the third person. He described a teenage boy who lived with his parents and two older sisters, all of whom pampered him. This boy had never been to school yet his parents taught him to read at an early age. He then taught himself German at twelve in order to read Kafka in the original. He loved corduroy and although he hated to shop, professed a love for fashion.

But that was his only non-literary passion. The rest of the time Maurice was absorbed in reading, writing (he wrote poetry, although he never acknowledged requests for a sample), and taking long walks in the park near his house, dreaming up monsters for a long epic poem he intended to write. His parents rarely interfered with his activities, and during his sixteen years on earth he'd read more than anyone he had ever met.

In turn, Mrs. Lanska told him a bit about her own life. She had never married and called herself 'Mrs.' in order to earn more respect from the Society, especially the academics. There had been a stage, she wrote, when she was desperate to find a man and start a family, but as it never happened, she decided to create a mystical union with Kafka instead. So far this had kept her happy. She didn't mourn the absence of children, although every now and then she wondered how different life would be with a few little ones running around the house. But she had just turned fifty-four, she said, and it was too late.

Maurice proved exceptionally mature and insightful for his age. When Mrs. Lanska wrote to him of these things he would reply with long letters concerning the spiritual value of literature, and how books – as much of a cliché as it was – were better company than most human beings. One had to be selective with friends, less so with books. A book that was not satisfying could be shut and returned to the shelf. It was slightly harder to get rid of people.

Mrs. Lanska could not have agreed more, and their correspondence soon evolved into a misanthropic outpouring against the world in which they two were the only ones who met the high standards they set. She began to distance herself from everyone, screening calls from friends, family and members of the Society. Before long, she forgot she was writing to a sixteen-year-old. Details of her private life crept into her letters. If she embarked on a new diet, she would outline her three meals a day. Moved by something she'd seen on television, she would recount the entire plot, sex and all. If she'd been to the doctor and he'd discovered a new allergy, she'd tell her pen pal.

Maurice began disclosing more information as well. He told Mrs. Lanska about his favourite foods and enclosed sophisticated recipes for fish and pasta. He also told her about the Bergman cycle he had just watched, and she was astonished by how such a young lad could understand the complexity of the relationships in those films. It was not until this letter that she decided to ask his age once more.

Maurice did not respond for a day or two, and then sent a long letter in which he ignored the question. Mrs. Lanska's suspicion rose. She asked again. Maurice did not write back. It occurred to her to drive to the town where he lived. Yet when she called directory, his family was not listed. The following afternoon she spent four hours going through every piece of correspondence she had received from him. There were no clues as to his age, but she began to suspect she had been fooled by an adult who was having a laugh.

Mrs. Lanska decided to bring an end to the correspondence, a difficult decision given that it had become her only source of solace . . . And to think she'd been hoodwinked by a member of the Society.

A few mornings later, the young postman knocked on her door and brought in a large blue package. Mrs. Lanska's heart quickened a beat as she tore away the string and tape. The blue paper revealed a box, and inside the box she found the book of Kafka stories she had sent Maurice. Attached to the jacket of the book with a paper clip – carefully, so as not to harm the cover – was a note written in flourishes:

Dear Mrs. L,

I am sorrowed and perplexed as to why you have not replied to my last missive. I can only assume that you have decided, for reasons unbeknownst to me, to terminate our correspondence. It has been the most important correspondence of my life and I shall be sorry to end it. But I respect your decision and as such, I return the Kafka book you so kindly sent me when I was still in your favour. Should you ever consider resuming our dialogue, please do not hesitate.

'How much my life has changed, and yet how unchanged it has remained at bottom!'

Yours most sincerely, Maurice G.

It had not taken much to tip the balance back in his favour:

Dearest Maurice,

Forgive my silence, I shall speak of it later. Meanwhile, I do hope you can attend the annual Society meeting, which is to be held at the Town Hall next week. If you cannot afford the fee, you may attend for free. Should you have any further queries, I would be most happy to address them.

Kindest regards, Mrs. L

Maurice did not reply to her letter, yet she assumed the silence indicated he was planning to come. Her mind was too aflutter to focus on practicalities, so she delegated most matters to Jenny Horn, the Secretary of the Society. It was Jenny Horn's duty to ring up all the members and confirm their attendance. It was also her duty to visit the Town Hall and test the acoustics, visit the two delicatessens that were to provide sandwiches and, lastly, guarantee the supply of Kafka books for sale. During the last annual conference the Society had run out of bilingual editions of *The Castle*.

The week dragged on. Mrs. Lanska found herself waking up in the middle of the night with a start. She, who had sadly remembered few dreams in her lifetime, was now experiencing such vivid ones she could scarcely stay asleep. The dreams all involved moments from her childhood: her life at school, feuds with her brother, long afternoons in the park. Her life pre-Kafka, uninteresting to anyone but herself.

The meeting inched closer. Mr. Howells, the Vice President of the Society, who in those days probably read more

Kafka than Mrs. Lanska, gave Jenny Horn strict orders to show him each confirmation slip that arrived. His enthusiasm could not be contained when members wrote to confirm their attendance, and he would run through the office squealing. Seventy-four people had accepted so far and they were waiting to hear from at least ten more.

Finally, after striking the days from the calendar hanging in her office, Mrs. Lanska was startled to see the conference looming one day away. She began to think about her wardrobe, something she had never paid much attention to in the past. Yet Maurice would probably dress elegantly for the occasion and she wanted to match him.

No one understood why she was leaving at three – especially when there was still work to be done – but she insisted it was important. Ms. Horn in particular was distraught to be left on her own, but Mrs. Lanska promised that Mr. Howells would deal with all eventualities.

Clusters of boutiques lined the small, cobbled streets, and she wandered through the fashion district uncertain where to enter. Finally she was drawn to a lilac awning beneath which stood a lanky girl with teased-out hair like a rag doll. Mrs. Lanska told her she needed a dress for a very important conference.

Within minutes Mrs. Lanska found herself in a narrow dressing room surrounded by eight dresses of varying lengths and colours. The music playing in the shop made her feel youthful, and she plucked a pink taffeta dress from the hanger. It fit well, but not perfectly. The sleeves were too long and the cut was awkward, emphasising her piano-leg shins. She removed the dress and grabbed the next one, a purple-and-black affair with mutton sleeves and a high collar. This proved to be more flattering and she set it aside. The next few dresses did her no favours, so she put the second one back on and stepped out of the dressing room. The rag doll rushed over and told her how elegant she looked, and how there was no doubt that that was the right one. Mrs. Lanska fished out her credit card to pay. For a second she considered charging the dress to the Society, but decided against it. It was time to separate her private life from Kafka.

That night she made herself a pot of chamomile tea and re-read the four Kafka stories which Maurice had listed as his favourites.

At breakfast she could hardly eat a thing. All she could think about was the prospect of meeting Maurice, once and for all. Nothing seemed impossible now. Her entire life she had waited to meet someone who not only loved Kafka but who saw the world the way she did. She blotted out the fact that he was perhaps a few years, even decades, younger. After all, hadn't her dentist just married a cardiologist twenty-five years his senior?

She slipped on her purple-and-black dress and smoothed her hair back into a chignon in order to highlight the collar. A few sprays of perfume, a change of shoes, and she was ready. Another layer of lipstick was applied as her cab negotiated the early morning traffic. No calls had come in from the office so she assumed everything was under control.

After paying the driver, Mrs. Lanska got out and joined the people climbing the stairs to the old Town Hall. Most of them were in black, so she concluded Maurice was either inside or had yet to arrive. Someone called out her name. It was Jenny Horn, dressed, she noticed, in a rather dreary grey suit. Ms. Horn told her that seventy-seven members had now accepted, and that a few more were certain to appear unannounced.

The hall buzzed with activity. To the left of the entrance stood a table covered in name tags, though Mrs. Lanska's heart sank upon seeing there was no Maurice G. among them. Well, no matter – he would probably turn up at the last minute. She walked into the main hall and past the seated members. Most people had already taken their places and sipped from paper cups of coffee while balancing notepads on their laps. She realised how important this conference was to Kafka readers around the world. And the list of participants that year was impressive: distinguished scholars and literary figures had been recruited from both sides of the Atlantic, from as far as Sydney, Vladivostok and Buenos Aires.

A hush fell over the room as she climbed onto the podium. All eyes fixed on her and for the first time ever she relished the attention. Somewhere in the room there would be a new set of eyes, watching with particular interest. Mrs. Lanska smoothed back her hair and cleared her throat before addressing the guests. First she thanked them for coming. She said that Kafka readership around the world had reached an impressive level; no one should fear that he would ever be forgotten. There were now more literary journals devoted to him than to nearly any other writer in the German language, save perhaps Goethe and Thomas Mann.

Mrs. Lanska promised the programme for that day would be first rate and offer much to ponder. Halfway through there would be a one-hour lunch break. At the day's end, once all the talks had been given, the panel would be opened to discussion. The audience murmured in approval.

Before introducing the first speaker, she would read through the list of participants. Just as she began, she noticed a small commotion at the entrance to the hall. But all eyes were on her, so she continued:

Dr. Juno Howett: *Investigations of a Dog: Animal Symbolism in Kafka's Stories*

Ms. Letty Brears: *Kafka's Neurosis as Literary Trope*

Mr. James Cusk: *The Real Truth behind 'The Great Wall of China'*

Dr. Mortimer Booth: *Nabokov as Reader of Kafka*

Dr. Christina Frei-Londig: *Kafka and the Talmud*

Mrs. Ana Truarte: *Psychoanalytic Incursions into Kafka*

Dr. Jean-Philippe Grèze: *Mapping the Unmappable in 'The Castle'*

Mr. Marco Palatti: *Kafka in Love: 'Letters to Milena'*

Dr. Vanessa Thomson: *Light and Shadow in Kafka's Three Novels*

Dr. Sacha Notovsky: *Fragmentary Digressions: 'The Blue Octavo Notebooks'*

Mrs. Lanska had just finished reading out the last item when a high-pitched voice called to her from the other end of the hall. It was not a familiar voice. She strained her eyes in its direction. All she could see, if her eyes did not betray her, was a small figure in green struggling in the clutches of two tall men. Ms. Horn came running down the aisle between the dozens of seats and scrambled onto the stage. Seconds later, she was at her side, pulling at her sleeve.

'There's a dwarf down there who claims you invited

him, free of charge, to the conference!' she whispered in her ear hysterically.

'What are you talking about?' Mrs. Lanska asked, her body tensing.

'Come see,' Ms. Horn implored.

Mrs. Lanska introduced Dr. Juno Howett so hastily she said 'Howells' instead, and clambered down behind her assistant. They crossed the room with quickened steps, two pairs of heels click-clacking down the aisle. Distracted by the sound, a few members of the audience turned as they passed.

When Mrs. Lanska reached the commotion her suspicion was confirmed. Standing there, or rather squirming, was a very small man in a forest-green suit. He wore a toupee and a bright yellow tie with flying saucers. His face was not unpleasant, although at the moment it was twisted into an ugly scowl. His head reached the height of her breasts.

The dwarf said her name. The high-pitched voice belonged to him.

'Maurice?' Mrs. Lanska asked.

'Of course,' he answered. 'You promised I could attend the conference for free. Have you forgotten your promise?'

She made a sign to the two men to release him. Once out of their grasp, Maurice straightened his suit.

'I was not expecting such a warm reception,' he said.

'And I was not expecting such a young, robust man,' Mrs. Lanska replied.

'Well, what did you expect? A child prodigy?'

'You misled me.'

'You misled yourself . . . I love Kafka, isn't that enough?'

The two pen pals stood staring at each other. Ms. Horn watched from close by, debating whether to interfere.

'Take a seat, then,' Mrs. Lanska sighed, before rushing back to the podium in time to introduce the next guest.

All things considered, the rest of the conference went smoothly. By dint of some preternatural strength, Mrs. Lanska managed to block out the uncomfortable incident that started the day. She did glance down the aisle a few times, but tried to focus on the lecturers' brilliant exposés, reminding herself of her love for Kafka and how that love superseded all other emotions in her life.

Dr. Christina Frei-Londig's presentation was especially good, and Mrs. Lanska felt pleased for having insisted on the eighty-two-year-old scholar. There had been all kinds of complications with the ticket from Buenos Aires and in the end the Society had had to pay extra for Dr. Frei-Londig to fly in Business, but it had been worth it.

During the lunch break Mrs. Lanska did not stray into the public and asked Ms. Horn to fetch her sandwiches and coffee. Ms. Horn followed orders but was confused; in the past, the President of the Society had loved to mingle with the guests. But not today. Today Mrs. Lanska remained by the podium, repeatedly straightening out her dress and smoothing her chignon.

The conference resumed ten minutes late. Some guests, unable to stomach the sandwiches on offer, had stepped out in search of a restaurant.

It was only towards the end that Mrs. Lanska's hands grew clammy. Her eyes scoured the room and she thought she could see a small figure in green sitting at the back to the left. In fact, she was quite sure there was a figure in green at the back, and that this figure had not shifted his gaze from her since morning.

Mrs. Lanska asked Mr. Howells to give the closing speech, which he did with pleasure. She could tell he was basking in his new responsibilities.

And that was that. Thrilled by the outcome, Ms. Horn and Mr. Howells came up to hug Mrs. Lanska. The less shy scholars approached her too, to thank her for inviting them to such a distinguished affair. All of this took place while Mrs. Lanska stood on the podium.

After shaking hands and imparting a few smiles, she stepped off and nearly knocked over her pen pal, who was waiting below.

'Can I have a word with you?' he asked, steadying himself on a nearby chair.

'Of course you can.'

Mrs. Lanska excused herself from her colleagues and followed Maurice down the aisle. She could not help sighing when they reached the hall.

'What are you sighing for? What's wrong? Has something dreadful happened that can never be made good?' Maurice asked mockingly.

Mrs. Lanska stared at the small man for a moment before answering.

'You must have had a sorry childhood.'

'I weigh my past against my future,' he retaliated, 'but find both of them admirable, cannot give either the preference.'

'What exactly are you trying to say? Are you having a laugh?'

'Yes, of course I've been playing a comedy! A comedy!

A good expression! What other comfort was left to a poor old widower?'

Mrs. Lanska took a few steps back before screaming, 'Will you stop quoting Kafka, goddammit!'

Nearby, a few members spun their heads around. Here was the President of the Society, right after a hugely successful conference, reproaching someone for quoting Kafka!

Maurice stood very still. 'Yes, we're both in the right, and to keep us from being irrevocably aware of it, hadn't we better just go our separate ways home?'

'I can't think of a better idea,' Mrs. Lanska replied, and began walking towards the exit of the building. Maurice ran ahead. She moved to one side but he puffed out his chest and stood in the doorway.

'Get out of my way!' she snarled.

Maurice's scowl lifted and for a second he looked sad. Stirred by pity, Mrs. Lanska moved towards her pen pal in a gesture of reconciliation. Maurice took a step towards her too. All of a sudden his face lunged forward and, through the dress, he bit into her breast.

Mrs. Lanska yelped.

The dwarf unlocked his jaws and moved away. She stared at him in disbelief. Then she began to feel a strange, tingling sensation deep within her body. After all, her breasts hadn't been touched in years. But before she had time to say anything, Maurice clapped his hands and ran out the door. Dazed and bewildered, Mrs. Lanska stood for a few seconds massaging her breast. All that remained was a dark circle of saliva. Ms. Horn came running up.

'Is everything all right, Mrs. Lanska? I saw that little man flying out like his pants were on fire.'

'Everything's fine,' she muttered.

'Well, then, we were wondering whether you'd like to join us for dinner? Some of the scholars are hungry.'

'Well, I'm not. And I'm not coming into the office on Monday either. Tell Mr. Howells he can take over. I know he's been wanting to get into my shoes for many a winter now. I'm leaving.'

Ms. Horn's eyes swelled. 'Where to, Mrs. Lanska?'

'I'm going to investigate whether there are any openings at the Robert Walser Society,' she cried as she ran down the steps of the Town Hall, the mutton sleeves of her dress denting in the wind.

Museum of Night

As a lifelong insomniac, I have for years envisioned a Museum of Night, a kind of metaphorical extension of what happens in my mind while the rest of the population is asleep.

The walls of the museum would be grey with glowing flecks of white, the light dimmed to a twilight tenor. There would be nothing unusual about the space yet it'd seem elastic, as if uncertain how to accommodate its inventory. Which includes:

1. A long glass showcase full of movement. It is a terrarium filled with fluttering moths. There are also large black nocturnal flowers, from which the moths emerge – a petal folds in two, breaks away from the centre and flies off. Some of the moths have golden eyes on their wings, others are a dusty grey. They flap about in different directions, their wings folding and unfolding darkness. Occasionally a light-bellied moth settles on the glass pane, the X-ray of a dream, a still from a nightmare.

2. A 12 × 20 × 15-foot cardboard construction, four black walls painted with streetlamps. On one of the walls, a sign:

CITY OF DREADFUL NIGHT
A VICTORIAN NIGHT WALK
AS EXPERIENCED
IN NINETEENTH-CENTURY LONDON

Beneath the sign, printed by Hamburg and Humbug Holograms & Dioramas Ltd., a paragraph describes the adventure:

Every city has its nocturnal wanderers, people who stumble about bleary-eyed, desperate for distraction or repose. Daunting avenues that endlessly unfurl and dark scratchy corners where couples cower. Towers and bridges, knots of tension and neurosis. Solitary travellers, like strayed migratory birds, confronting a vastness without coordinates. Every route is limitless. At night infinity takes over and there is no difference between a castle and a prison.

3. On a shelf, a metal box with windows, meters and dials:

NOCTURNOGRAPH
DEVICE FOR MEASURING NIGHT
(PATENT PENDING)

The machine records various aspects of night. A fluxometer measures degrees of stillness. This is done through the detection of sound frequencies and movement down to the slightest stirring. Attached to the left side of the Nocturnograph is a barometer. A tiny sea of mercury rises halfway in the slender glass tube, indicating placid minutes in the museum. Another feature measures the depth of night, calculated by registering the textures and patterns of darkness, which vary depending on the size of the space they inhabit. But the most intriguing aspect of the machine is its capacity to measure shadows. It claims to record the exact time at which shadows come into being and predicts how long they will remain in existence:

Some shadows are thicker, others more opaque, some denser, others more fluid. Everything depends on the time of afternoon or evening they were born and on how long they have been in existence. Novices (shadows recently created by rearranged objects, new compositions) need to be reminded when to appear and are nudged into being by their elders, who monitor the sun's movements as they prepare themselves for the moment they will slip into view.

4. A sheet of parchment under glass. Undated. Anonymous.

'Excerpt from Memoirs of an Insomniac'

Word spread long ago that my mind runs on a twenty-four-hour schedule and that even more space is available here at night. Once the sun has retreated and the moon has entered the sky, all kinds of boarders come a-knocking in search of company and asylum. Occupants arrive and depart before I have time to inspect them, their presence announced by a quick bow or tip of the hat or tail, but on the whole they are too absorbed in their colonisation to care much for etiquette. Vast unexplored territories are claimed and populated before I have time to investigate. Maps are useless, as are citizen registries; as long as I remain awake there are no borders or frontiers, quotas or restrictions.

Just as one does not choose to pass a sleepless night, one cannot select the denizens of one's imagination, especially after dusk. And the faster my thoughts multiply, the greater the number of individuals who rush in to set up tent. How convenient for those who prowl the early hours, detached from shadows and banished from the realm of sleep, to find an unbolted door. Some band together to form a community of discarded fears and fantasies, of the debris that doesn't even make it into dreams.

Only once I drift off do the creatures pack up. Some brought little baggage to begin with and simply throw their capes over their shoulders and set back into night. Others need more time to gather their things and summon their brood. With sleep the attic doors bang shut, at least until the following night, when the influx and immigration resume.

Notes on the International Lightning Strike Survivor Conference

There are three types of lightning: cloud to cloud, or intercloud, which leaps across gaps of clear air; intracloud, which doesn't leave the cloud at all; and cloud to ground, the most threatening: a stream, or rather a meeting of two streams, of ionised particles, each following its own determined course, one towards the heavens, the other towards earth, and where they meet the air crackles with heat, creating a sky of forking paths.

To the attendees of the International Lightning Strike Survivor Conference, who have all had encounters with the third kind, the oft-mentioned statistic (nine out of ten survive) offers little consolation. Many of them, given the consequences, would prefer to have been struck dead. Survival provides small solace when your entire existence has been electrically altered.

Just as lightning isn't a single event but rather a sequence of strokes, so the memory of a lightning strike returns in fierce, dramatic bolts rather than as one clear picture. Among the attendees of this lightning strike survivor conference, held in the Hudson Valley, in the state of New York, the weekend of 17–19 April 2009, a few individuals are especially eager to share their story:

EINAR GERHARDSEN, a tall musician of thirty-six, had been sitting on a hill in the outskirts of Oslo watching a motor race. The cars buzzed past like angered wasps, the red leading the way. After the red came a green and then a blue, flashes of colour streaking the tarmac. And then an altogether different kind of flash, this one more luminous, less metallic. At first Einar thought a bomb had gone off. Nearly one hundred spectators were thrown from their seats and scattered across the hill. People shrieked, the cars continued to zip by, engines louder than human cries. Minutes later sixteen ambulances, nearly as fast as the race cars, appeared. Half the spectators, Einar included, were loaded onto stretchers and taken away.

Einar advances in small steps and has an uncomfortable relationship with the ground. He prefers stairs and inclines and, like a tightrope walker, feels lost when confronted with too much flat surface. Prone to panic attacks and overwhelming bouts of confusion, he never goes anywhere without his mother. There are no physical traces of the strike yet his mind is a maze of short circuits.

The distinguished ornithologist ALEX COSTA from Tampa, Florida, the lightning state (three times more strikes than any other in the United States), was observing a rare migratory bird when struck, and when he returned to his senses the bird had vanished along with his shoes, binoculars and long-term memory.

Indoor landscape painting (he rarely leaves home) has replaced ornithology and, with his good hand, he now paints imaginary woods and meadows. He doesn't sleep much at night but reads and takes long naps in his armchair by the window.

MARJORIE WINTERS, a dark-haired woman of fifty-six, survived the strike but her terrier didn't. At around midnight Arthur was let out for a final run, and she was on the porch having a last cigarette, when all of a sudden something crackled and popped and Arthur let out half a squeal. When Marjorie stepped off the porch to investigate, a second strike flung her across the garden.

Now she's a collection of nervous twitches and tics, her body and brain inclining heavily towards the left, and she's had to have her pacemaker replaced twice. She has also lost the ability to feel the cold and needs a thermometer to dress. Arthur, meanwhile, lives in a cabinet with glass doors, his legs bowed under, jaws petrified in mid-yelp. After two thousand nights sleeping at the foot of her bed, he's now curled up like the dog of Pompeii.

Twenty-nine-year-old CHARLES WINLAKE is a walking lightning rod. Already struck four times in his brief life, he fears the sky has yet to leave him alone. His first experience was in his early twenties, as he drove along with his elbow propped out an open window. The second time, two years later, it happened while opening the tap of the kitchen sink: a massive bolt outside, an electrical current travelling up his arm. The third time, he was meditating beneath a tree (by then, he'd turned to Buddhism). And the fourth, just under a year ago, occurred when returning from an amusement park. All four times, his heart stopped beating for nearly a minute.

He's added rubber soles to every shoe and replaced his metal-rimmed glasses with plastic frames but each time he leaves home he glances upwards with trepidation. His dream to become a landscape gardener is long over and he can't concentrate on anything for more than a few minutes. His speech is slurred, his hair gone grey, headaches blinding. Apart from two pet salamanders, his prized possession is a fulgurite, the hard, mineral imprint of lightning's path underground (a glass tube of petrified lightning), which his cousin once found up on Mount Thielsen.

MICHAEL and PETRA UEBERMEYER had been sitting in folding chairs listening to a summer concert played by students from the local conservatory – 'ein ästhetisches Tortur', according to Michael – when lightning struck from above and wiped out the cellist and lead violinist. It also hit the audience in the first few rows. Michael later accepted all physical and psychological consequences as penance for having criticised the young musicians during the last seconds of their lives. His wife, however, who had avidly supported the quartet, saw no reason to be philosophical. Both received permanent cobwebbed wounds on their sides and Michael, a musicologist, was left deaf. He spends his days reading musical scores or else walking up and down his street with a weary step.

Crustaceans

My very first glimpse was from above, from the vantage point of my bedroom window: a wide-rimmed purple hat, a sliver of black, a long, thin arm extending in the direction of the doorbell. And then, seconds later, the bell – once, twice, a third and fourth time – before the arm withdrew.

For reasons that weren't clear until much later, I had never met my grandmother Benedicta before that September in 1995. After a while I'd almost forgotten she existed. Every now and then, once or twice a year at most, my father would mention his mother in a quiet, reverential tone, but the conversation was always shifted to something else before I had time to ask any questions. Some topics – my mother's first husband, my father's suicide attempt and Benedicta – were best avoided.

Yet one evening, to my surprise, my father brought her up at dinner, and this time no one tried to change the subject. He picked up his napkin and twisted it round and round until it was soft enough to tear into shreds, a sign that an uncomfortable topic was on its way, and once the shreds could be shredded no further, he spoke.

'My mother needs money . . . She needs to sell the house in New Brunswick. A telegram arrived today.'

My mother sat up in her chair, her shoulders tensing as she reached for her glass of water.

'This time it's serious,' my father added.

'Why?'

'Don't know the details, but she needs money.'

'How much?'

'She doesn't say. But she needs cash. Urgently.'

'Well, you have Dieter's address, email him and have it transferred.'

'Should I do that or can you?'

'There's no reason why you can't. He's your friend, not mine.'

'He's my accountant.'

'And friend. Your *only* friend.'

She was right. My father had only one friend in the world, one remaining friend, that is, and his name was Dieter Korb. Long ago my father had many friends, but over the years he shed them like trees shed leaves in autumn and now there was only one remaining leaf, one little leaf clinging to the branch – more out of stubbornness than genuine affection, we felt – and that perennial leaf came in the weathered shape of the seventy-five-year-old accountant Dieter Korb.

From one day to the next, my father had stopped seeing people. Without warning he quit his job as fact checker at the local paper and decided to start following the stock market from home. From one day to the next, digits and decimals replaced faces and voices. At first it was simply a matter of turning down invitations to dinner parties, office parties and picnics, but before long he would dash to his bedroom each time he heard the phone or doorbell. Yet his days of dashing were limited; pretty soon the phone and doorbell stopped ringing.

If my father's world shrank by ninety-five per cent, my mother's world shrank by about eighty. She still kept in touch with one or two of her oldest friends, went to the movies (alone, unless I accompanied her), walked our dog until it died and twice a year visited her sister Liza in Los Angeles, but there was no question her world had also been greatly, dramatically and, as it seemed at the time, irrevocably reduced. One day a cloud of little white moths flew out of her favourite dress and it wasn't long before she discovered that more than half her clothes were infested. She moved everything to a trunk, filled it with balls of naphthalene and slid it under the bed.

By the end of the first year of his 'withdrawal from the demands of society', my father had whittled down his excursions until all that was left were the post office and the supermarket, and those only on days when he was feeling a touch confident and assertive. Even on occasions when he agreed to come to the A&P he would linger a few steps behind the trolley while I unloaded the items and my mother dealt with the cashier.

I'd never paid much attention to the word 'pathological' until one afternoon when I overheard my mother whispering it into the phone. 'He's pathologically shy, I tell you . . . It's definitely pathological.'

And then, a few minutes later, 'No, Liza, trust me. It's pathological. You need a crane to hoist him out of the house.'

By the third repetition of the word I realised that my

father's shyness was there to stay. It was 'pathological', and with such a clunky word attached to him, he was marked for life.

Two nights later, the subject of Benedicta came up again at dinner.

'Another telegram has arrived,' my father mumbled.

'Speak up, I can't hear you,' my mother said.

'Another telegram.'

His first napkin in shreds, my father reached for another. 'It . . . seems she has nowhere to go.'

'Mmmhmm.'

'And, well, she asks if she can come stay with us. You know, just for a while. Until she works things out.'

My mother laid down her fork. 'She wants to stay *here*?'

'Yes.'

'But how could she possibly?'

'Why not?'

'Well, to begin with, Daniel is busy with school. And you have to start earning again.' – 'I will,' he interjected. – 'As for me, well, I have my hands full, just looking after the two of you.'

'She won't get in our way, I promise.'

'How do you know?'

'She'll keep to herself, as she always has.'

'You know how I feel about her.'

'It might change once you spend time together.'

My mother turned to me. 'What do *you* think, Daniel? How do you feel about having your gloomy grandmother Benedicta come to stay?'

'I've never met her, I don't know.'

Her arrival, two weeks after the last dinner conversation, was announced by an impatient ringing at the door. After glimpsing her from my bedroom window I ran down to open it with a pounding heart. Here was my last surviving grandparent, the woman who had brought my father into the world, the very embodiment of that mysterious topic so often avoided at dinner. The doorbell began to ring again, even more furiously than before, as I pulled the latch.

How to describe Benedicta? She was, in many ways, indescribable. Before I met her, the name had given rise to visions of a pious old woman with flushed cheeks and of wide circumference. Her actual bearing, however, could not have been further from my fantasy. She was thin and brittle and pale as wax. Her face was long and gaunt, her lips dry and her eyes small. You could tell she was not used to smiling.

I relieved her of her two heavy suitcases, which emitted a rather dank smell, as if they'd just been fished out from a basement after decades of disuse.

'Benedicta!' My mother emerged from the living room and opened her arms. She was making an effort.

Benedicta recoiled so abruptly she bumped into the wall behind her. 'Where's my son?'

My mother withdrew her embrace. 'He's out in the garden. Should I fetch him?'

'Just show me where he is.'

Too shaken and intimidated to speak, I pointed in the direction of the garden. Without another word, she brushed past us, pausing only once to straighten a painting that for as long as I could remember had hung crooked on the wall.

I will never know what took place during that first re-encounter between mother and son, but minutes later my father entered the house, laid his giant shears on the table and, grabbing a suitcase in either hand, led Benedicta up to her new room. They climbed in silence, my father leading the way, and re-appeared an hour later, for dinner.

That evening my mother served carrot-and-ginger soup, a tray of roast vegetables and a large slice of salmon. She even opened a bottle of white wine and filled everyone's glasses halfway.

'So, welcome to our little home,' my father said. We raised our glasses and clinked.

'Thank you.' Benedicta took a small sip and set her glass back down.

The breadbasket was passed around while my father went to fetch the salt and pepper shakers from the kitchen.

Once we were nearly done with our soup, my grand-mother spoke, her voice much less brittle than the rest of her.

'They should be wiped out.'

'Excuse me?' my father asked.

'They should be wiped out.'

'Who?' asked my mother.

'The Serbs.'

'Have some salad,' my mother said, extending the bowl.

'No, nothing green,' Benedicta replied. 'And nothing solid. I'll stick to soup.'

'Well, the air strikes continue,' my father said softly.

'Nothing but soup?' my mother asked. 'There's vegetables too.'

'No, just soup. I'll finish what's left and if you don't mind, I'll have more soup tomorrow.'

'Not even mashed potatoes and things like that?'

'Must I say it a third time? Just soup.'

My mother ladled what was left into her bowl. Benedicta thanked her with a nod.

'But not all Serbs are to blame,' my father ventured even more softly, but no one reacted.

Soup, three times a day. Prepared fresh by my mother each morning. Heavily salted soup, usually cream of mushroom or Jerusalem artichoke (*topinambur*, as she called it), both as pale as her face. And when my grandmother wasn't lifting a spoon to her mouth, blowing when it was too hot, she would sit at the table and stare.

It wasn't until the second week that the staring began, or at least until I noticed it. One afternoon after school I was on my way to my room to drop off my bag when I began to feel odd, as if someone were watching me. At first it seemed like no one was around but then I caught sight of two eyes peering from between the hinges of Benedicta's door, which lay slightly ajar. I pretended not to notice and quickened my pace. The eyes were still there when I passed on my way back downstairs. This seemed to happen nearly every time I passed her room.

Despite the staring, my father had been right: she certainly kept to herself. My mother commented on the fact she saw Benedicta even less than I did, and I spent half the day at school. Not that she minded, of course. And on the rare occasions when my grandmother wasn't cloistered away, she would be in the basement doing laundry. Laundry seemed to be the only activity she enjoyed, at least beyond her room, and there were days when she would spend hours down there, ironing shirts, nightgowns, trousers, napkins, tablecloths, curtains, bed linen and whatever other item in the house could possibly develop a crease. She'd keep the iron on the highest temperature and was especially fond of the steam function, my mother reported, mountains of moisture rising out as she pressed down.

One evening at dinner Benedicta clamped down on her spoon a little too enthusiastically and chipped a molar. It took nearly a week for my mother to convince her to see a dentist and another week to convince my father to accompany them, but in the end I witnessed the not altogether unwelcome sight of the three of them packed into the old Volvo, my mother and Benedicta seated in front, my father, shielded by his cap, in the back.

Now was my chance. For nearly eight months – had she really been with us that long? – her room had remained a mystery. I looked out the window to make sure the car had driven off, then headed straight to my destination. An aggressive smell like turpentine enveloped me as I opened the door, though I couldn't figure out where it was coming from. I switched on the overhead light and looked around. My grandmother was rather tidy, it appeared, certainly tidier than any of us. The twin beds were perfectly made, the sheets fanatically smooth, every surface as if polished.

The closet lay open, revealing a row of woollen dresses in a range of colours. I'd never seen Benedicta in a single one but there they hung, the whole spectrum, the red dress between the orange and the yellow, the blue between the green and the black. Beside the dresses was the black woollen coat she'd arrived in. I sensed it wouldn't be worn again until her departure.

I was about to explore more deeply in the closet when my attention was drawn to a row of pint-sized jars, some with lids, along a shelf at the far end of the room. I walked over and held one up. Unless my eyes were playing tricks on me, there were tiny things, almost microscopic, swimming around inside. It might have been a play of light. I switched on the bedside lamp and shone it in the direction of the jars. Even with the added illumination their contents were too small and translucent to identify, but something was criss-crossing the water in tiny squiggling motions. Just holding the jar made me nervous. I set it back down on the shelf.

The jangling of keys, voices downstairs. I quickly turned off the overhead light and stepped out, softly closing the door behind.

At dinner that evening my grandmother sat across from me, her face so pinched she could barely fit a spoon through her lips, and whenever she did manage to get it in, she would slurp her soup in the most loathsome way. I wondered whether it was the dental anaesthetic they'd given her or simply a progressive pinching of the face, but the sound was torture. I directed my thoughts elsewhere, namely to the jars in her room. Were they medical samples? An arcane drug or a magic potion? Whatever Benedicta was up to, the thought of her harvesting anything made me determined to find out more.

A few Saturdays later, our town experienced the fiercest rain on record. Curtain after curtain of water, rattling the roof and the windows. The damp and the cold finally caught up with my mother and she collapsed in bed with the flu. My father had no choice but to look after things himself. That weekend he drove me to the nearest shop to pick up a gallon of milk, waiting in the car while I jumped out to make the purchase.

'I think Benedicta is hatching something,' I said to him on our way home.

'Oh yes?'

'The other day I happened to go into her room and saw a whole row of jars on the shelf. There were small transparent things swimming around inside.'

My father did not reply. Nor did he comment on the fact I'd gone into her room.

'Well?'

It was far from the reaction I'd been expecting. He didn't pull the car over to the side of the road, he didn't even flinch. He just kept driving.

'It seems my mother has returned to an old pastime of hers,' he simply replied.

'Which is?'

'I'd rather not go into it just now. But it's best if you keep this from your mother. There's no need to upset her over such a minor thing.'

'Well, but what is it?'

'It's nothing to worry about, Daniel, trust me.'

As I lay in bed that night, I realised I was completely in the dark regarding Benedicta's political sympathies, apart from her desire to bomb the Serbs. But what else could my father have meant by 'an old pastime'? The fact he wanted to keep it from my mother was suspicious, and I hadn't liked the look of those transparent creatures.

One Saturday morning the doorbell rang three times. My parents were still in bed so I ran down to open the door but to my surprise Benedicta was already at the door, a raven in her grey-and-black gown, being handed a pile of envelopes.

'What's that?' I asked as the postman pushed off with his cart.

She closed the door and headed back upstairs, clutching the pile.

'Isn't there something for us in there?'

'No, Daniel, it's all for me.'

'Everything?'

She didn't answer, just continued upstairs, and when she reached her room she closed the door and did not emerge until after dinner, for the first time skipping all three meals.

As the weeks went by Benedicta grew more secretive. And obsessive. She stared over breakfast and lunch. She stared over dinner. She stared from her window when I came home from school. She stared when I walked past her room to mine. But she said nothing.

On 4 November, Yitzhak Rabin was assassinated by an Israeli settler. That same week, negotiations in the former Yugoslavia began in Dayton, Ohio. By the end of November, a peace agreement for Bosnia had been reached. Not that Benedicta took notice of anything by then, not even of developments in the Balkans. Apart from the moment when I returned home from school, I don't think she looked out the window. She grew more and more withdrawn as the months wore on, and there were times when I wondered what would happen once I went off to college. No one ever spoke of finding her another home and I was under the growing impression that she was there to stay, as permanent as my father's pathology.

She began missing meals even more often. Usually she would appear for breakfast, but on some days she would skip all three and leave her bedroom only to use the bathroom across the hall. Her sole outings were to the post office, from which she would always return with a hefty pile of mail. As soon as she returned she would march up to her room and shut the door, her message more powerful than any lock.

One night I was already in bed with the lights off when my mother knocked and took a few steps into the room.

'You've seemed quite anxious these past few months,' she said, her voice expanding in the dark. 'Are you scared you won't get into college?'

'No, it's not that.'

'Then what's troubling you?'

The moment had come.

'Close the door and I'll tell you.'

I turned on my bedside lamp while she closed the door and came to sit on the edge of my bed.

Without omitting a single detail I told her about the staring, which she said she'd noticed too, and the row of jars in Benedicta's room and the huge stack of letters the postman had delivered. I told her I thought Benedicta was part of a cult or conspiracy but that when I'd mentioned all this to my father he had attributed her peculiar behaviour to 'an old pastime.'

When I'd finished pouring out my worries my mother took a deep breath and said, 'Benedicta used to stare at your father a lot too, when he was a boy.'

'How do you know?'

'He told me once, long ago.'

'And then what happened?'

'Nothing. She thought it was good training. It's an odd

theory of behavioural psychology, which her mother also used on her. Discipline through intimidation.'

'Are you sure? She stares at me *all the time*.'

'Do you really think we would allow her to live here if we thought she posed a threat to you in any way?'

'But she stares *all the time*,' I repeated.

'Yes, I know. There's nothing to worry about, Daniel. It might be odd, but it's not threatening in any way. It's just disciplinary.'

'But I don't even need to be disciplined!'

Without addressing this last point, my mother went to fetch my father, who entered shortly afterwards with heavy steps, his arms and head drooping like an old bear's.

'Alan, could you please tell us what us what you meant by "an old pastime"?'

'What are you talking about?'

'Remember, Dad, that day in the car when you told me that Benedicta had returned to an old pastime?'

My mother got up to close the door, which he'd left open.

'Well . . .' he began, then stopped.

'Dad, you said it *was* something.'

'Well,' he started again, 'my mother is prey to a bizarre folly. But it's not dangerous, don't worry.'

'What do you mean?'

'Well, it's just a little bizarre. Nothing to worry about.'

'Tell us,' we pressed him.

'It's just some mail order thing from long ago.'

'What do you mean?'

'Sea monkeys,' my father mumbled.

'Sea monkeys?' I wasn't sure I'd heard right.

He nodded.

'Sea monkeys?' my mother repeated.

He nodded again.

'I thought they were for kids.'

'They are. Usually. She began when I was in my twenties, right after I graduated from college and went back home for a year. That's when they first came out. I remember she sent away for the whole shebang. She even ordered a wristwatch with sea monkeys swimming around inside. She'd keep them in jars in the kitchen, right by the sink, next to the sugar. First they were on the windowsill, then she moved them to the piano, a bowl on a piano no one had played in years. And then one day, we never knew why, she flushed all her sea monkeys down the toilet and that was that.'

'Horrible,' my mother said. 'Actually, what exactly *are* sea monkeys?'

'They're those little critters you get mail order, who wear tiny crowns and live in underwater castles,' I said, recalling the colourful ads I used to see in comic books.

My father laughed, a rare sight.

'No, Daniel, they're hybrid shrimp eggs that remain in a state of suspended animation until they're placed in water, and then they hatch. Instant pets, they say.'

'Where do they come from?'

'They're scooped up from dried-out lake beds.'

'So they're not even from the sea.'

'Nope, and they sure ain't monkeys, either.'

We laughed, though it wasn't funny.

'How come you know so much about them?' my mother asked.

'My mother was addicted to these things. It was impossible not to pick up a few facts.'

'But what does she do with them?'

'I guess she watches them . . . Apparently one can hypnotise the critters, though I think that's just light manipulation. And there's even an aphrodisiac you can send away for, which encourages them to mate.'

'So that's what she has in those jars?' I couldn't help feeling a nip of disappointment.

'I'd imagine so. Unless they're invisible goldfish, another mail order invention from the same guy. The invisible goldfish come with invisible food and a guarantee their owner will never see them.'

Once it had been clarified what Benedicta was up to, her presence bothered me less. She still gave me the creeps, but at least I knew she wasn't casting spells or turning military on me. Let the old lady have fun with her sea monkeys, what did I care. I just didn't understand why she had to be so secretive, or, for that matter, why she insisted on 'disciplining' me.

One day after school it occurred to me to knock on her door. After all, she *was* my grandmother, and most people I knew spent time with their grandparents. The knock was hollow, as if the room were empty.

'Who is it?' a voice called out.

'It's Daniel.'

'Yes?'

I could hear the voice move closer to the door.

'I just wanted to say hi.'

There was a pause.

'What exactly is it you want?'

'To come in and say hello.'

Another pause.

'One moment.'

I heard the sound of shuffling across the room. The closet sliding shut. Eventually the door opened and there she was, backlit by the lamp on her bedside table, in a blue knit dress I'd never seen before.

'Come in,' she said, stepping aside so I could enter.

From the very first glance I noted that all the jars had been removed from the shelf, not one in sight.

My grandmother eyed me curiously.

'Are you looking for something?'

'No . . . it's just that I never come in here.'

She stood very still, between the bed and the closet, without offering me a seat. Her dress hung loose around the waist.

'So, Daniel, how is school?'

It was the first time she had ever asked.

'Fine. I just hope I get into college.'

'You will.'

'Are you happy here, Grandma?'

The question came out of nowhere. I hadn't been planning to ask and I'd certainly never called her Grandma before.

She didn't answer immediately, just placed a hand on the back of the chair without leaning on it and sighed.

'Am I happy here? Why should I be happy here? Are *you* happy here? Nothing in this house inspires me . . . This house is a swamp.'

'What do you mean?'

'There's no air.'

My legs began to hurt though I'd only been standing a minute or two.

'Don't you know what a swamp is?'

'Yes, I do.'

'So there's no need to explain.'

The silence grew heavier.

'Well, I guess I'll go now.'

'Very well, Daniel, goodbye for now.'

And so our feeble bonding session was brought to an end.

Like most people faced with an uneasy but non-threatening situation, my parents carried on with their activities. On most days I would find my father glued to his computer and my mother cleaning, fixing, tweaking, as if in anticipation of imaginary guests. The house never looked elegant enough, she said, and every few weeks I'd notice a shift in the layout of the furniture downstairs, like the red sofa that now faced the door rather than the fireplace, or the two green chairs from the dining room that from one day to the next were deemed too plain and demoted to the kitchen. No one ever helped her move the furniture because she never asked for help. I don't think my father even noticed the changes in the layout, and as for Benedicta, she rarely set foot in the living room.

In December the Dayton Peace Agreement was signed in Paris, ending three and a half years of war in Bosnia. In our town, four inches of snow fell in two days and our basement froze over. Once school vacation started I focused on finishing all my college applications, my head buzzing with visions of another life.

Benedicta was eating less and less. It struck us she was growing thinner, although it was hard to tell since she'd begun wearing a baggy purple sweater. Often her cream of mushroom soup was left unfinished, only the foamy top layer spooned off.

'Eat, Mother,' my father would say.

But Benedicta would push away her near-full bowl and mutter the same words she'd first spoken to me: 'Nothing in this house inspires me.'

One night after dinner, exactly two months before my graduation, Benedicta announced she was leaving. My mother and I leaned forwards. My father's mouth fell open. She explained she was going to go and live with some relatives in Maine, a pair of aged cousins, both widows, who ran a donkey sanctuary. Why she hadn't gone to Maine in the first place was another story, but this was, without a doubt, good news. She added she no longer felt comfortable in our home and had 'things to attend to'.

'A bit of fishing or farming, perhaps?' my mother couldn't help asking.

Benedicta smacked her lips, making a funny suction sound.

'Tell us why you're leaving,' my father implored. 'Aren't you happy here?'

She cast me a glance. I couldn't see how I was in any way responsible. She still stared often, but I couldn't imagine she expected anything from me or had been disappointed in my behaviour. My one visit to her room had confirmed that. Perhaps it was true she was up to some odd disciplinary mischief. Whatever the reason, she seemed set on her decision.

'Mother, tell us,' my father pleaded.

Benedicta laid down her napkin and this time looked him straight in the eye. 'It's the atmosphere in this house. I can't breathe. Nor can anything else.'

'You can't breathe?'

'No, Alan, I can't . . . I have to leave before I suffocate.'

'Well, perhaps we could change your room, give you the study with more windows. Or Daniel's room once he goes to college. But what's so bad about where you are? I just don't understand.'

She didn't answer.

'Does it get in the way of certain activities?'

'It's none of your business what I choose to do in my spare time.'

After pronouncing these words she rose from her chair, pushed in her seat and left the dining room.

The next day when we woke up she was gone. None of us heard any sounds in the night. But her room was empty, the door wide open and all the jars had vanished. Not a trace of her remained aside from the smell of turpentine, which my father attributed to a storage or cleaning solution for the sea monkeys. Later that day we discovered a note on the table in the corridor, asking us to please forward her mail to an address in Maine.

So, Benedicta left. My mother was relieved to see her go, my father visibly disturbed and I, I felt angry. As far as I was concerned, she had imposed her moth-eaten self on us for nearly ten months, upset the calm of our house and then left in indignation.

'You see, Alan,' my mother would say, 'it's this stagnant atmosphere, even your mother felt it . . . This house is a sanatorium, stuffy and removed from the world. I don't blame her for leaving, I really don't.'

'You're happy she's gone, admit it.'

'Maybe I am.'

A few months after her departure my father wrote to the address Benedicta had left, inquiring into her well-being. He received a laconic reply, from one of the cousins: 'Benedicta is well. She sends her regards.' He stuck the note, written on the back of a postcard of a fir tree, on the fridge.

My father even braved the phone two or three times. But she never picked up, and when, much to our surprise, he suggested visiting Maine, the aged cousins immediately wrote to dissuade him on the pretext it might unnerve their nervous, timid donkeys.

She died a year later. A printed card with black borders arrived in the post. No details about the burial or a will, simply date, place and, as if anticipating our question, the word 'pneumonia' handwritten. My father tried calling but the cousins never answered. After the announcement, we never heard from them again.

It wasn't until long after this that I felt ready, or rather, permitted, to enter her room. Of course I'd been curious to explore since the day she'd left, but something like superstition had always held me back. Every once in a while my mother went in to dust and open a window, but we kept the door closed. Door closed, topic closed.

I was home for the summer after an unexceptional freshman year. On my second evening I announced I would like to go and explore 'the room'. My parents exchanged glances and then said fine, as long as they could accompany me.

The air still smelled of turpentine, the beds still the way

Benedicta had last made them, the lace-covered pillows side by side, their lower halves tucked under the blanket. The shelves were empty, as was every other surface in the room.

'Old Benedicta,' my mother sighed, placing a hand on her hip as she looked around.

My father sat down on the bed. He gazed at the pillows and their lace covering. He was missing his mother.

The closet door was open, exposing a row of empty hangers where Benedicta's coloured dresses once hung. As I drew closer, I spotted something on the top shelf at the back. I dragged over a chair and climbed up. The inside of the closet was dark and I could hardly see a thing but I stuck my arm in deep and prayed there weren't any spiders. My fingers hit against something. I grabbed onto what felt like a handle and pulled out one of the suitcases Benedicta had brought with her.

'Incredible,' my mother murmured.

'I guess she left it behind,' my father said absently.

'Well, it's too late to forward it to her.'

I laid the suitcase on the bed.

'Not on the bed, on the floor! It might be dusty,' my mother cried out.

'What are you doing?' my father asked.

'I want to see what's inside. Don't you like to know what you have in your own house?'

I unbuckled the sides of the suitcase and opened it. Hundreds of bright green envelopes came spilling out. I held one up. SEA MONKEYS, the print on the envelope said.

'Sea monkeys,' I read out loud.

'Sea monkeys,' my father repeated.

My parents crouched down on either side of me as I

ran my hands through the suitcase. Most of the envelopes appeared to be empty, but others contained little heaps of tiny, dried shrimp eggs waiting to come to life. Beneath the pile of envelopes were a couple of empty jars, a bowl, a spoon and a small jar of Tabasco sauce. I lifted the spoon.

'There's some dried stuff on it, look.'

The spoon was passed around for inspection and I think we all had the same thought at the same time. My mother was the one who said it out loud.

'Benedicta was eating those poor sea monkeys. She was just gobbling them up, who knows how many a day . . . I guess my soup wasn't good enough for her.'

So, that's the story of what happened to me and my family the year before I went to college. Of course a lot of other things happened too, but those were the highlights. My roommate Jim here doesn't believe me when I tell him I had a gloomy grandmother who ate sea monkeys, or a father who was too shy to ever leave the house. He also didn't believe me when I told him that my mother walked out on my father shortly after I returned to college for my second year. She said she'd been waiting for 'centuries' to do this, and once I was gone for good there was no need to stay on. Her time there was up, she said. As for my father, he still spends his days at the computer, but now that he's on his own he has no choice but to visit the supermarket every now and then and stock up on provisions.

My mother claims she is much happier. Maybe she is. She definitely talks and laughs a lot more and gallivants around town in her patched-up suits and polished jew-ellery. Her new boyfriend is a policeman, one of the top guys at the local station, and she seems proud of him. We get along fine, Hawk and I. He has a smile fixed to his face nothing can erase. Even when he catches a delinquent or loses a colleague to the front line, he is smiling. My mother says Hawk was exactly what she needed, especially after my father began sleeping on one of the beds in Benedicta's room. One night he'd just carried in his pillow and blanket. That was bad enough. But when the first envelope of sea monkeys arrived in the mail, she knew it was time to leave.

In the Arms of Morpheus

Insomnia has a boomerang effect.
You can never fling your thoughts far enough.
Before night is over, they have returned to lodge more deeply.

For as long as I can remember, my local health food shop has shared a wall with Route 81, the Hell's Angels headquarters of East London. Two ideological strongholds, each proposing a means of survival in our corrosive urban world, and as far as I know a neighbourly relationship exists between the two, provided the organic shoppers respect the motorcycles on the sidewalk and don't stare too long at the bearded titans colonising the benches outside.

While Route 81 offers a whole range of piercings and tattoos at painless prices, the health food shop always has a stack of free leaflets on hand. Mostly these offer information about yoga classes and baby-care facilities, but occasionally there are others, catering to the more adventurous or unhinged.

At the shop one morning my attention was drawn to a shiny black brochure emblazoned with a full moon, at whose centre was written:

TIRED OF WRESTLING WITH SLEEP?
Victorian Sleep Laboratory
Free Consultation. Free Trial Night.
Guaranteed Results from Highly Trained Analysts
Call or Drop by: 89 Hardware Street, NW3
Telephone/Fax: 8878 2940

I had no plans after work so I decided to visit the sleep
laboratory that very evening. I'd always been wary of this
kind of research, of letting others tread where you yourself tread so vaguely, but my insomnia had hit an all-time
high and I'd lie awake at night when even the ghosts were
snoring. Rules like 'No ticking or luminous clocks by the
bed, especially those electric ones with loud digital numbers' followed me from home to home. The size of the bed
mattered too – to sink into a vast black sea rather than a
shallow, waveless pond where you could see straight to the
bottom – and I'd recently traded in my futon for a large
mattress. Yet no matter how comfortable the bed or how
silent the place, my mind refused to rest.

Of course I'd tried sleeping pills, and couldn't deny
their allure: one tablet and the rest of your night would be
purged. You could watch horror films, summon anxious
thoughts, drink a double espresso; no matter what, sleep
would ensue. And yet they were no silver bullet. You'd remain trapped in a grey zone, see-sawing between mid- and
shallow slumber, mind and body switched off but not of
their own accord. There was simply too much indecision:
should they follow the commands of this foreign signal or
trust their own intuition? Should they wait until night had
fully set in or shut down early, ignoring the promptings of
the circadian rhythm? Whenever I took a pill I'd feel like a

timid guest lingering at the threshold, waiting for an invitation to enter, an invitation that always failed to arrive. I would see what the people at the sleep clinic had to offer.

The lion's-head knocker, coated with a thin layer of rust, groaned when I banged it. A man in blue overalls opened the door.

'Hello, I've come for a trial consultation,' I said.

He didn't answer, just held the door open wider and led me up to the office on the first floor, modestly furnished with one long window facing the street. To the left of the entrance hung a life-size poster of Charles Dickens astride a stool, a glazed expression on his face and a pendulum dangling from his right hand.

Nearly all the desks were occupied by what I could only imagine were sleep technicians. Some scribbled in notepads, others stared into space; most looked under thirty. A man with an unkempt beard and a tweed waistcoat rose from a desk at the back. Judging from his confident manner, it was he who ran the show.

'Hello, I'm Dr. Sheire. What can I do for you?'

'I'd like a free consultation.'

'Do you suffer from insomnia?'

'Most nights, yes.'

'Well, you've come to the right place. Take a seat,' he said, motioning to a chair. I sat down, removed my sweater and draped it over my lap.

'So tell me, how long have you been in night's clutches?' He studied my sweater as if it might provide insight into the problem.

'I don't remember. Maybe all my life.'

'Well, we should be able to help you. You can spend the

night at our clinic for free, while we monitor your sleep rhythms. If things go well, you can sign up for a month's trial at discounted rates. Now tell me, do you have a student credential?'

I shook my head.

'No matter. First I will ask you to fill out our questionnaire.' He opened a desk drawer and extracted a yellow paper, which he passed to me.

'Now, pick a night.'

There seemed little point in waiting.

'How about tonight?'

Dr. Sheire pulled at his beard. 'Well, there is another patient coming in, but I don't see why that should be a problem.'

At a desk nearby, a male assistant nodded in agreement.

'Tonight, then . . .' the doctor resumed. 'We recommend having a light supper. Nothing too heavy, it'll cause sleep disturbances.'

'Should I bring pyjamas?'

'No, we have everything here . . . And we prefer patients to wear our robes. Just bring a toothbrush. By the way, how much caffeine have you had today?'

'One cup of tea in the morning,' I said, glossing over the other two lest he disqualify me.

'Perfect. That shouldn't be a problem.'

Just holding the questionnaire produced a sense of calm, as if the sheet of yellow paper could sail me through the haziest of waters.

'If you don't mind my asking,' the doctor resumed, casting another glance at my sweater, 'do you take sleeping pills?'

'Sometimes.'

'That's what I thought. I've had many people come in here with either dulled minds or puffy faces, sometimes both.'

I raised a hand to my cheek.

'Don't worry, neither is permanent. But you should dispose of your pills when you get home.'

'By the way, why is the clinic called a Victorian Sleep Laboratory? Do you use nineteenth-century techniques?'

Laughter from the desks around me.

'No, no, on the contrary. Here we have the latest in sleep observation . . . We simply liked the name and since night was an important time for Victorians – Dickens went on many night walks, you know – we thought we'd pay homage.'

Dr. Sheire pulled out a pocket watch and flipped it open. 'It's nearing seven. Why not come back at nine? With the questionnaire, of course.'

The form, filled out at my kitchen table, took half an hour to complete. The majority of questions came as no surprise: How long had I suffered from insomnia? What were the symptoms of my ailment? Was I of a nervous disposition? Any traumatic experiences in the past? Exercise regime? How much tea or coffee per day? Cigarettes? Sex? Self-pleasure? Would I spend most nights alone or accompanied? And then, towards the end, a string of odder questions: Did I sleep with the door to my room open or closed, and if open, how many centimetres? How many years had I owned my pillow? Any plants in the house I occasionally forgot to water?

Beneath the glow of the streetlamps the clinic's facade looked old and worn, wearier than at dusk. A stab of anxiety. I considered turning back. After all, no one was forcing me to spend the night in a foreign bed at the mercy of strangers. Yet something propelled me onwards – the agony of my most recent sleepless nights, not to mention my dwindling supply of sleeping pills – and before long I was once again banging the lion's-head knocker. The same man in blue overalls opened and led me silently up to the office, where Dr. Sheire awaited. The other desks had emptied and I wondered whether the sleep technicians had gone home to their families or been zipped into cocoons at the back.

Dr. Sheire's eyes zigzagged across the page as he read my answers to the questionnaire. A female assistant appeared. Without looking up he said, 'Maria will now check your pulse and heartbeat.'

Maria, a stern young woman with blond hair jerked into a bun, led me down the corridor and into a room with two leather armchairs, a long mirror and a counter with a few medical utensils.

'Take a seat.' She motioned to a chair and with grave silence took my pulse and listened to my heartbeat.

'Your pulse is normal; so is your heartbeat. You're a lucky girl.'

Dr. Sheire strode in just as Maria was removing the stethoscope from around her neck.

'So,' he turned to me, 'would you like to see one of the machines that will be watching you tonight?'

The neighbouring room was crammed with boxes, steel cabinets and outlandish machines that seemed to vary greatly in age. Some looked like the latest model in sleep observation and others antediluvian, with wooden knobs and spokes that protruded a foot from the base.

Dr. Sheire paused at a three-foot-long rectangular contraption and tugged at his beard. 'This is a polygraph, which records your brain waves. See these little pens on top? Well, once you begin sleeping they will scratch away, and then this paper here will roll out, illustrating the pattern of your brain waves. I know what you're thinking . . . how can such a clumsy piece of machinery pick up on the subtle movements of the brain? Well, trust me, it does!'

He pulled open the drawer of a steel cabinet filled to the brim with coiled metallic eels capped by white barnacles.

'And here are the wires and electrodes that connect you to our machine . . . with the help of a special gel.'

'Cold?'

'Not at all. Well, maybe a little.'

In the main room Maria stood holding a blue cotton robe. She passed it to me and then dropped her hand to her hip, awaiting further orders.

'Ah yes,' Dr. Sheire continued, 'here is your gown for the night. It facilitates the electrode business. Maria will show you where to change.'

Marvelling at the immobility of the tight bun, I followed her down the corridor to the changing room, which was much like the first room but without the armchairs or mirror. I removed my shoes and hung my clothes on a peg on the door. The blue robe, soft and airy, was fitted with a thick belt.

On my way back to Dr. Sheire I became aware of footsteps coming towards me from the other end of the corridor. Not the stern steps of Maria or the brisk, confident ones of Dr. Sheire. These steps were hesitant and slightly overcast, and they announced a tall, slender young man with a pale, oval face and bags under his eyes like a Russian icon. He wore a grey sweater and black jeans, though I noticed a blue robe, similar to mine, tucked under his arm. I glanced at him as he walked towards me, then down at the floor, then back up at him as he drew nearer. He shot me a searching look as we passed, surprised, surely, that there was company. His footsteps faded into the floorboards as he entered the changing room.

'So, have you met our other patient?' Dr. Sheire asked when I returned.

'Not yet.'

'Well, it's his first time too so we'll wait until he's ready and run through the programme together.'

Wrapped in a pale blue robe that fell to just above his knees – he must have been a good six feet tall – my fellow patient appeared minutes later. His shins were almost translucent.

'Come meet our other insomniac. For reasons of confidentiality we won't say your names, but now you are acquainted.'

Our eyes met for a second, then quickly parted.

Oblivious of the bizarre climate he was conjuring, Dr. Sheire clasped his hands and said, 'Let's run through the programme.'

Everyone was now seated, symptom bearers on one side, symptom reader on the other.

'First, you will spend an hour or so in the sleep preparation room, with its selection of journals and herbal tea. We suggest you avoid entering into conversation, however, since conversation before bed leads to a surplus of new thoughts . . . And once you're feeling sleepy, we'll lead you to your room.'

'Our *room*?' I asked.

'Well, yes, it is indeed one room. I'm sorry, but as you can see this is not a large enterprise. There'll be a curtain separating the beds, so you needn't worry . . .'

Sleep, I realised, would be an impossibility that night.

'. . . and once you're both lying calmly in your beds we will attach our friends the electrodes to your face, back and underarms. The electrodes are then connected to the polygraph. You'll each have your own. And then lights out, as you are carried away in the arms of Morpheus while my assistants and I monitor your brain waves from next door.'

His words were met with silence.

'Oh, and I should mention the two small cameras on the ceiling that record external movement. Tossing and turning, sleepwalking, things like that. You will each have a bell by the bed in case anything is needed during the night. Any questions?'

Still processing the information, I shook my head and out of the corner of my eye saw the other patient shaking his head too.

'Well, off you go!'

The man in overalls led us to the sleep preparation room, a dimly lit space with sofas and round tables. At the centre, a coffee table with stacks of magazines, mostly of a scientific nature – *The World of the Brain, Journal of Neuroscience, Scientific American, Neuron, Proceedings of the Royal Society*. I picked up the latest issue of *Scientific American* and took the sofa nearest the door. After selecting a magazine from the top of a pile, the young man chose a sofa at the opposite end of the room.

'Now, which tea would you like?' the sleep technician inquired. 'We have peppermint, chamomile, rosebud and verbena.'

I asked for peppermint. The other patient lifted his hand in a 'no thank you' gesture before shifting his gaze back to the magazine.

A few minutes later, my tea was brought in in a yellow mug.

'We're next door if you need anything,' the sleep technician said. 'You should think about going to bed within the next hour.'

I looked at my watch. It was approaching ten. Time passed quickly in the clinic.

'Is that a watch?' the technician gasped.

'Yes.'

'Well, I'm afraid watches are absolutely forbidden here. They are the enemies of sleep.' He held out a hand with bitten-down nails. 'If you don't mind, I'll put it in the other room with your clothes.'

I unbuckled my watch and entrusted it to the sleep technician, then returned to my magazine. Apart from our quick exchange of glances in the corridor, the young man had yet to look in my direction.

Forty minutes later, or perhaps thirty, the man in overalls re-appeared and summoned us to bed.

Not until I stood up and instinctively tightened the belt around my waist was I reminded of what I was wearing. I pulled at the hem and smoothed out the top to add some definition but it was useless: a robe is a robe. At least I wasn't the only person wrapped in one.

Our room had a low ceiling and two beds, four feet apart, each flanked by a table with a glass of water and a bell. A heavy grey curtain, waiting to be drawn, hung bunched between the beds. The place was even more clinical and confining than I'd expected; nothing worthwhile, I was sure, would emerge from such a vacuum.

'You're first,' Dr. Sheire announced to the other patient, patting the bed on the left. 'And you,' he said, turning to me, 'we'll fix you up in a couple of minutes. Why don't you lie down meanwhile?'

I chanced a final peek, one last image to put by for the night, before the curtain was pulled. The other patient sat on the edge of the bed, legs crossed and hands in lap, his robe cracked open, revealing a hairless chest. This time he was looking over, directly at me. A sheet of grey sliced our room in two.

Only once the curtain was drawn did I notice the small surveillance camera peering down from the right-hand corner of the ceiling. Its eye was pointed in the direction of my bed and I imagined its twin watching from a parallel corner of the room. Minutes passed.

Eventually Dr. Sheire emerged from behind the curtain, followed by an assistant wheeling the table of wires and electrodes. They stationed themselves by my bed and the assistant began coating each electrode with gel before handing it to the doctor, who attached them, one by one, to my forehead, chin, above each eye and behind each ear. I was asked to turn over so that more could be applied to my back. The electrodes were weightless but clammy, like the embrace of a small swamp reptile. Once everything was in place I was hooked up to the brain-wave machine, which another assistant had wheeled in on its own little table.

'So, we're recording three things tonight,' Dr. Sheire explained. 'First, your REMs, then electrical activity in the brain and, finally, any muscle movement . . . If you need anything just ring the bell. Bon voyage.'

Once the doctor and his crew had left, I took a few sips of water. Just as I set my glass back down on the table, the room fell into total darkness, as if the contents of a giant inkwell had tipped over. I turned onto my side. An electrode dug into my temple. I turned onto my other side. Another electrode. As I searched for a comfortable position I imagined Dr. Sheire and his men crouched around the polygraph waiting for us to shut down. But what was going on beyond the curtain? Was he awake, was he asleep, was he touching himself? What was his name? Did he own a dog? How many people had he kissed? The clinic bed was hard and unyielding and the pillow smelled of cheap detergent. And yet, somehow, after countless turns during which I cursed my three cups of morning tea, I fell asleep.

It was hard to gauge how early I woke up but judging from the stillness it must have been before eight. Without a window in the room it was impossible to tell. I glanced into the other section as I reached for my glass of water. The grey curtain was drawn, the bed empty. A coil of electrodes, still attached to wires, cascaded over the side.

The gadgets must have alerted Dr. Sheire to my shift in consciousness. 'Good morning. How are we today?'

'Fine, I think.'

'Now tell me, how many hours do you think you slept last night, total?' His eyes radiated a manic light and I wondered whether he himself had slept.

'What time is it now?'

'Seven thirty-three.'

In bed by eleven, up past seven, minus the time it took to fall asleep.

'Around seven?'

'Actually, you slept for exactly five hours and thirty-eight minutes.' He searched my face for a reaction. 'You woke up nineteen times in the night, though I'm sure you don't remember. At one point you were awake for a whole five minutes. But I'm sure you don't remember.'

'No...'

'On most occasions you were awake so briefly our machine barely registered a note, but if you string together all those fallow moments they add up to half an hour, which we must subtract from your night.'

'Was it at least deep sleep most of the time?'

'Well...' Dr. Sheire unplucked two electrodes from my forehead. 'You spent quite a while in Stage Two. That's not deep but it's real sleep, unlike Stage One, the slippery state between sleeping and waking. Stage Two takes you further. Then it's Stage Three and Stage Four, the deepest sort. All movement is down, down, down... Now, please turn over.'

He lifted my robe and removed more electrodes from my back. Once they had all been unsuctioned Dr. Sheire's assistant wheeled away the table and machine. I was released. The floor of the changing room was a thin sheet of ice. I dressed hurriedly, my thoughts still far away, though I wasn't sure where.

'So, your sleeping patterns are rather interesting,' said Dr. Sheire when I returned to the main room. He was sitting very straight, back columned with chair.

'Just out of curiosity,' I began, taking a seat across from him, 'what happened to the other patient?'

'Ah, the other patient. Every now and then we have a coward who reneges.'

'He left?'

'That's right. Now tell me, aren't you surprised that you only slept five hours and thirty-eight minutes?'

'Would you mind telling me his name?'

'All our patients' names are confidential. I'm afraid I can't give out any details.'

'Not even a name?'

'Certainly not. Now, shall we return to the matter at hand?' he asked, tugging at his beard. If he tugged it one more time I would tug it for him.

'About the way I slept?'

'Tell me, do you remember anything from the night?'

'Not really.'

'Nothing at all?'

'No, not really.'

'Any physical sensations, for example? Feelings of discomfort, any twitching or tingling?'

At that moment a little brown moth flew past Dr. Sheire's head. Without a second's deliberation he rolled up his stack of papers and began to swat at it. He didn't stop until he'd thwacked the tiny creature and sent it tumbling. I thought I could see a smattering of moth dust.

' . . . I might've had a dream.'

'A what?'

'A dream.'

'I see. But you must know, of course, that dreams are nothing more than electrical discharges. You shouldn't pay much attention to them.'

'But . . .'

'It's important for you to distance yourself, as soon as

you wake, from your dreams. Don't let them linger. Contrary to many schools of thought, there's little porosity between conscious and unconscious states.'

'I think . . .'

'It is the dreamer's narcissistic drive to believe that dreams are individual, tailored to all the little dramas in your life. Well, the data I'm about to share with you will soon prove otherwise . . .'

'I think I'd like to go now,' I said, glancing down at the small, winged corpse by Dr. Sheire's notebook.

'What do you mean? We're just getting started.'

'I'm sorry, but I need to go home.'

'Don't be offended by our positivist approach. Trust me, you will sleep much better once you accept that night is no more than [I covered my ears] and that dreams are no more than [I covered my ears again].'

I rose from my seat. 'I think I should go now.'

'You know, we don't give out free trials just like that . . . Incredible, two duds in one night . . .' Dr. Sheire muttered as I walked to the door.

The city was still awakening as I buttoned my sweater and started on my way home from Hardware Street. A chill in the air, encouraged by a mounting wind. The garbage truck had yet to make its rounds; large bags of rubbish cluttered the sidewalk. A man in a dark blue suit bounded down the steps to his house, two at a time, while fixing his tie. Another man appeared, tugged along by a powerful Great Dane. Two children walked past with bright lunchboxes. I reached the bus stop and pulled out a cigarette. It took three matches to light. The bus pulled up after I'd taken only a few drags so I made a sign for the driver to move on. As I neared the end of my cigarette an incredible hunger took hold of me, a hunger I hadn't known in years, and I wandered around until I found the nearest café.

Years later, as I lie beside my snoring husband, I still wonder whether the person of my dreams had been that silent man at the clinic.

Nail – Poem – Suit

A man walks down the street trying to recollect the final lines of an unfinished poem he had been composing two nights ago when the phone rang. It was his seventy-four-year-old mother calling to remind him of the suit she'd ordered for his birthday, now ready for collection at the tailor's, although it was likely alterations would have to be made. He reaches the corner and treads on a large corrugated nail that goes rolling off the pavement and into the street. The man's first thought is that this nail has fallen out from somewhere inside him; his second thought is that it dropped out of the woman wheeling a bicycle a few metres ahead. His third thought is that the nail fell out of the teenager with the pierced lip who delivers the post each morning. Unable to draw any conclusions, the man casts one final glance at the nail now lying parallel to the tire of a parked car and returns to the matter of the unfinished poem, which, should he ever complete it, will surely fit him better than the tailor-made suit.

World Weather Report

Iceland: A strong low poetic system will lead to metaphor and potentially damaging similes across Iceland today. The strongest metaphors will occur on the southwest side, where they could gust past their referents at 60 kph (40 mph). Allegory totals upwards of 2 cm can be expected.

Germany: A geometric front stretching east and north from large quadrilaterals centred over Berlin will bring the threat of extreme angularity. Damaging fractals, torrential axioms and even isolated zeros will be possible from Cologne down into Bavaria.

France: Vigorous symbolism will continue to bring threat of shipwreck and heavy mermaid showers in several locations.

Hungary: A Cimmerian front stretching east and north and giant owls hovering over Budapest will bring a rash of ancestral thunder. Intermittent candlelight, unidentified accents and even isolated Bluebeards will be possible from Vác down to Hódmezővásárhely.

Mexico: High pressure from underground will create significant craquelure throughout the country. Increased moisture in the south will lead to expansion and contraction depending on temperature. Spiral cracks in the north due to extreme tension on surface, corn-ear cracks in the southeast due to sliding pressure. Meanwhile, a white powdery front moves in from the southeast towards the north border.

Russia: A Suprematist front will be stretching from northwest to southeast, with heavy abstraction bringing possibility of artistic purity. Black spells, chromatic silences and occasional rain of wolves will be experienced from Saint Petersburg to Vladivostok.

Essays

Into the Cosmos

Sometime during the summer of 1986 I went with my family to see a circus version of Mikhail Bulgakov's *The Master and Margarita* in an outdoor theatre in Kreuzberg, West Berlin. My only memory of the production is of Margarita herself on a trapeze, her laughter vampish and defiant as she sliced the air above us. By then we were nearing the end of the Cold War, though at the time no one knew it, and right there in a courtyard, metres away from the Wall, was this exultant and ephemeral expression of the conquest of space.

The conquest of space. The phrase comes up again and again as I sift through dozens of Soviet documents of the period. By 1986 the ardent years of the Space Age were of course over, its most notable vestiges a few space stations orbiting Earth, but the embers still retain a beguiling, and decidedly nostalgic, glow.

In East Berlin especially there has always been a great habitation of the sky: the television tower in Alexanderplatz, often beheaded by fog, the stately socialist buildings lining Karl Marx Allee, the less elegant, prefabricated tower blocks further east . . . That same summer of '86 I crossed Checkpoint

Charlie and in a bookshop on Friedrichstrasse, one of East Berlin's most important arteries, I met my friend Stefan. Born in Moscow, where he lived until the age of eight, he spoke, among other things, about his Russian grandfather Ivan Ivanovich Bryanov, who in the late fifties and early sixties had been doctor to the Soviet cosmonauts, endeavouring to cure them of their more terrestrial ailments.

And it was Stefan who, twenty years later when I was writing my first novel, accompanied me to Marzahn, in deep East Berlin, to research the area. As we drove down the Allee der Kosmonauten, one of its main avenues (there's a Cosmonauts' Alley in Moscow too), I remember expecting to see the huge faces of the cosmonauts looming overhead, as if chiselled from rock like the faces of the American presidents in Mount Rushmore, heroes from another epoch who silently, inscrutably, watched over their citizens.

Around that time Stefan mentioned that his grandfather, at age ninety-four, had just finished writing his memoirs, which included his experience treating the cosmonauts. He promised to show them to me one day, once he had finished translating them from Russian into German. As is often the case with the promise of a text one starts out by imagining, with no foothold on reality other than an intriguing description, the fantasies and secondary research it inspired proved to be more enthralling than the actual document. The longer I waited for Stefan to send me passages from the text, the more I dreamt of what it might contain, what strange, unsettling insights into the lives of these mythical cosmonauts would be granted.

Cosmonauts were considered the heroes of the Soviet Union: quite literally, they inhabited the stratosphere and then transcended it. In those fervently atheist times, it wasn't God or his angelic messengers who would come forth from the sky, but the cosmonaut. Yet the pressures were great, and the bars at Star City, the covert compound outside Moscow where they lived and trained, were populated by mostly gloomy individuals, drinking to either attenuate the powerful psychological jolt of space travel or else to face the fact they weren't chosen for any mission – the trauma of the experience or the trauma of a life unfulfilled. Despite years and years of training there was no guarantee one would be sent into space.

During the weeks I waited for Stefan to send me sections from his grandfather's memoirs, I conducted research at the library, forging my own tentative routes into the subject. I read or skimmed detailed aerospace medicine manuals, reports about the vestibular (inner ear) training of cosmonauts, some with graphs depicting sway data post-mission, studies in postural equilibrium and accounts of the physiological effects of such voyages, including headaches and tinnitus.

The most fascinating books were those that set out to explore, openly or in more figurative language, the psychological responses to space travel. They cover themes such as the side effects of weightlessness (loss of body sense and co-ordination, terror, confusion), the difficulty of long periods of silence, the emotional impact of outer space. One tome suggests applying the four humours to the process of task selection: the choleric individual is quick to learn but, prone to impatience, makes mistakes – therefore best for special assignments rather than routine ones; sanguine types flourish under variety and constant excitement rather than repetition (Gagarin was apparently one of these); phlegmatic types, on the other hand, are recommended for systematic activity; and melancholic types ... cannot become cosmonauts due to their nervous, fearful temperament, and are best suited to be scientific advisors on the ground.

Initially, it was unclear how man in space would react, how he would endure weightlessness and 'unknown nervous-emotional overloads'. In a pre-emptive move, a 'logic lock' was installed aboard the Vostoks – early Soviet spacecraft – to prevent any 'irrational intervention of the cosmonaut in the direction of the ship'. Gagarin, for instance, had no control over his voyage. After all, in this world man and machine were one, incorporated into a single control system, its two main exponents poised to operate at highest potential and coherence. Yet despite all the preparation, there were human variables, and the symbiotic relationship led to both real and imaginary ailments. One healthy cosmonaut, for instance, experienced cardiac arrhythmia after being exposed to sustained stressors related to onboard equipment failure.

During the first ninety-six-day Salyut mission in 1978, the cosmonaut Yuri Romanenko was apparently so mesmerised by the vastness of the cosmos that he stepped out to have a better look and forgot to attach himself with safety tethers to the space station. Fortunately his cohort noticed and quickly grabbed his foot as it floated out of the hatch. Even the most trained and disciplined individual could ignore all precautions and checklists and succumb to a greater urge.

And then there was the monotony of space, the long stretches of nothingness, whether experienced alone – certainly the deepest emptiness of all – or in a small group, when tensions nearly always arose. Despite the speed of the aircraft, inside there was often no sensation of movement and everything appeared fixed and motionless. Moments of sensory bombardment alternated with extended periods of sensory deprivation. The first few cosmonauts were given books; future ones, curiously, were instead handed knives, wood blocks, coloured pencils and paper with which to pass the time. Some individuals would apparently become so exasperated with the lack of stimuli that they'd wish for the equipment to break down simply to provide some variety.

Many cosmonauts claimed to suffer changes in spatial orientation, a lack of feeling of support, the loss of personality and, worst of all, a feeling of separation from Earth. Hard to imagine the experience of such severance, floating inside the capsule in a sometimes foetal position, the closest return to an amniotic weightlessness, yet at the same time violently detached from our planet, their only umbilical cord the electromagnetic waves of the radio and video transmissions.

As for the psychological aftermath, difficulties returning to everyday life were not uncommon. For this the Soviets created the Psychological Support Group for Cosmonauts to deal with in-flight problems and, particularly, post-mission malaise. During the flight, psychologists on the ground would closely monitor individuals via transmissions, analysing facial expressions, voices and behaviour, searching for tell-tale signs of stress. American astronauts, on the other hand, who had not been raised as atheists, often spoke of the experience as something profoundly religious and transcendent that transformed them forever, an altered state of consciousness leading to a spiritual awakening rather than an existential crisis. Seeing no need, perhaps, NASA never set up an equivalent to the Soviets' psychological support group.

Bryanov's memoirs, or rather four sections from them, arrived just as I was reading about the decline of the Soviet space age. From its twilight, I was sent back to its dawn.

Chapter VIII focuses on his years working as a doctor at the air force's central research clinic in Moscow, and describes how the launch of the artificial satellite Sputnik 1 on 4 October 1957 began a new era, 'the cosmic', fulfilling the prophecies of Konstantin Tsiolkovsky, the reputed father of Soviet space exploration, a notorious recluse with brilliant yet extravagant ideas, who by the late nineteenth century was already dreaming about interplanetary space travel.

In his memoirs Bryanov mentions the Baikonur Cosmodrome, the immense, secretive complex in the Kazakhstan steppe where the first test flights were launched, including Gagarin's Vostok 1. It remains a central launch pad to this day, leased by the Kazakhs to Russia until 2050. He also writes about the first living beings the Soviets sent into space: stray dogs, robust enough to deal with extreme situations. The ill-fated Laika was but one of many, though most of the others survived and were adopted by cosmonauts' families. When the time came to select the first man in space, Bryanov recounts, the criteria were broadened but remained essentially the same. Yuri Gagarin fit the ideal psychological profile: emotionally balanced, persevering, good-natured, in possession of a large vocabulary, creative, not fearful, contact- and decision-friendly.

Yet one week before his voyage, the twenty-seven-year-old cosmonaut walked into Bryanov's office and poured out his anxiety: his entire trip was in jeopardy, he said, for he had tremendous pain in his right cheek, the whole area was swollen, pus ran from his nose. 'Something's not right with me, please find out what it is.' The obliging doctor ran a series of tests – urine, blood, X-rays – and traced the cosmonaut's maxillary sinus inflammation to the ailing root of a tooth. A team of specialists debated what to do; treating the root would take too long. The tooth must be extracted, immediately. Other reports mention Gagarin was unusually laconic before his journey; behind all the bravado, one can imagine the fears.

As for Valentina Tereshkova, the first woman in space, she was personally selected by Khrushchev despite the team of doctors remaining unconvinced of her qualifications, for out of the five female candidates her 'vestibular-vegetative system' left the most to be desired. During her three days in space in June 1963 it was clear she was experiencing some hardship, though she kept insisting in her radio transmissions that all was fine. She was even out of touch for a while, prompting discussion at ground control as to whether to abort the mission. Back on air, she again insisted everything was fine. When she landed, however, she seemed visibly ill and upset, yet delivered a cheerful account and blamed her small lapse on a stale pierogi. Only later did she confide to Bryanov, 'How could I tell the whole group of superiors and the press, to whom I was expected to report, that I had a very hard time during the flight?'

The nautical suffix of 'cosmonaut' evokes the romantic image of a sailor of the universe, standing at the helm, the ultimate pioneer hurtling through space aboard his ship, propelled by the massive waves of elation on Earth. Yet as much as Soviet space exploration fed the illusion of freedom, it remained inextricably bound to the laws of physics and officials and, though to a far lesser degree, to the inner tides of human nature.

*

I returned to Berlin in 2003 and resided there until late 2008. Among my weekly rituals were visits to the handful of second-hand bookshops in my neighbourhood in the east. One of their many wonders was a slowly diminishing stock of publications from the USSR, including a variety of circus books. I found a collection of essays entitled *The Soviet Circus*. Printed in Moscow in 1967, its cover had a constructivist design depicting a faceless clown equipped with yellow cane and chequered hat, raising one arm in salute. Shaped from loosely fitted black, yellow and red geometrical forms, this two-dimensional cut-out had as much movement as anything fully rendered, a character assembled from colour and line.

In the introduction the editor described the rigours of training for the Soviet circus, commenting that the exercises (trampoline, etc.) were similar to those in cosmonaut school yet in practice even more difficult, since cosmonauts had more reliable equipment while circus performances depended on human strength and skill rather than on any mechanical device. The comparison immediately got me thinking about the parallels between Soviet cosmonauts and circus aerialists, the psychological fallout of both professions, the phenomena that would take place during and after a mission or performance, and the ways in which each embodied a collective dream, the reverie of everyday men, women and children projected onto these bodies in motion.

Like cosmonauts, aerial circus performers lead a kind of kinetic existence, almost entirely defined by motion, their identity bound up with spatial prospects and limitations. (Stray from your route – on spacecraft, tightrope or trapeze – and it may cost you your life. Stop moving – and you may die. Survival lies not in stillness, but in velocity.)

The modern artist – Jarry, Baudelaire, Picasso, Rouault – has often professed a strong affinity with the clown or acrobat, with their hyperbolised solitude, nostalgia or alienation, their wearing of masks and enigmatic detachment from society; could parallels not be drawn, too, with the complex nature of the cosmonaut? And what about vertigo, that very human affliction? In his essay 'On the Marionette Theatre', Heinrich von Kleist blames gravity and self-consciousness for impeding the graceful movement of the human body. I wondered about the psychological effects of weightlessness on circus performers. My friend Lara, a Russian writer in New York, put me in touch with two aerialists.

Vladimir Kekhaial performed in circuses in both the Soviet Union and Russia. When I asked him how much he distinguishes between outer and inner space, he replied: 'If we take it as a measurement, then humanity is zero point – the middle. It's called balance. We can go both ways but to a certain point only. Then the further we go, the more unattainable points we will see on the horizon.' As for outer space: 'Now, the Cosmos to me – that's the intelligent energy. It stays alive by vibration and everything in this material world has its own vibration. The gravity is part of that vibration.'

Masha Terentieva, by contrast, spoke about the euphoria of flight, the main reason people became acrobats, aerialists, tumblers – to experience that 'momentary conquest of gravity', a tremendous sensation of freedom and abandon when a centrifugal force pulls the body away from 'normal gravity'.

The collective dream of space travel, the individual dream of flying. Cosmonauts traversed regions that for the majority of humanity would remain at best imagined. Trapezists and funambulists inhabit a more accessible realm, yet one that also ultimately remains out of reach. They tower, soar or rush above us, populating the heights we can't, marking the distance from dreamer to dream.

In 1919 Lenin nationalised the circus, which, like space travel, also served certain political means and fostered patriotic spirit with folktales and lore. Performers of the state-run Moscow Circus School enjoyed great popularity, free childcare, retirement benefits and, best of all, the highly prized permission to travel. In our interview Vladimir remarked on how after the fall of Communism both the Russian space programme and the circus worlds suffered. Domestic focus, it seems, went from the vertical back to the mainly horizontal. They were indeed products of an age, and when compared to, say, American astronauts or circuses in the West, notions of flight and the overthrow of gravity were, inevitably, much more freighted with symbolism.

*

In Spanish, 'peak' (cima) and 'abyss' (sima) are distinguished by no more than a letter; is there much difference between the heights and the abyss? After all, are not flight and fall both physically and metaphysically intertwined? Gravity is much more than a physical force pulling us to the centre of the Earth; it holds our other systems in place as well, all that we have assumed as a given since birth. Remove it and you remove most existential certainty.

Free fall doesn't only suggest the chaotic downward movement exerted by gravity, or the drift of a spacecraft when the engines have been switched off. Nor is it limited to the moments during re-entry after the cosmonaut has been dropped from his aircraft and is parachuting back down to Earth, or the plunge of circus performers between high wire or trapeze and the net below. Free fall signals a more interior event, a momentary release from the tethers of our human condition.

The universe, they say, was born out of an explosion – perhaps there is an atavistic urge to replicate this outward burst, give it internal resonance, a return to the most primitive sources of energy. During rocket launch, cosmonauts paradoxically experience around three or four times the force of gravity; this tremendous pull is then followed by release, expanses of calm, a journey through dark matter, outside and within.

How to map this darkness? One might argue that in the

end both outer space and inner space are destined to remain shrouded in mystery and ultimately unknowable – and un-conquerable. We may undertake new voyages, assign co-ordinates, put names to the visible and the invisible, yet it is elusive territory to which we simply give form and mea-surement; wherever he finds himself, man's impulse is to limn his own mortal routes.

Kopfkino

For as long as I can remember, I have had a complicated relationship with sleep. I revere night yet am wary, greet its numerals with wonder and dread. Mornings bring relief, and the prospect of renewal; nights are far less predictable. My twilight hours are haunted by all kinds of spectres, and after a certain point these spectres acquire a physicality that's too voluminous to push to the back of the mind. What was kept successfully at bay during the day washes in in a noisy, powerful tide.

Whenever I seek assurance that my insomnia is not something that arrived with adulthood or even with adolescence, but rather much earlier in life, I return to a poem my father once dedicated to me: 'El insomnio empieza en la cuna' (Insomnia Begins in the Cradle). My sleepless nights began long before I knew the ailment had a name. My parents would peer into my darkened room and see me standing in my crib, gripping the bars and peering over the rim, waiting for something or someone to come and save me from the desolation. Decades later, I experience that same old resistance to laying the day down to rest.

In my family home in Mexico, to which I still return twice a year, night remains magical and mysterious, infused with a childhood reverie that has yet to expire. All it takes is a trip down to the kitchen at two or three in the morning, past the masks on the walls and the Indonesian puppets staring out at me – in every corner, a watchful eye – to be reminded that everything harbours a hidden inner life. These artefacts are more awake than any member of my family, and I feel abandoned by the living, who are, at that moment, incontestably further away.

Night also defies the passage of time. My old bedroom still holds the same familiar configuration of bed, bookcases, desk and closet as it did when I left home, and in the darkness the decades are instantly erased. The thoughts keeping me up may differ, but in that space – in that darkness – I am back to who I was at sixteen.

During various periods of my life I have succumbed to the siren call of sleeping pills. It is hard to resist their promise: one tablet and your night will be purged. Your brain may be in overdrive, its receptors working away, hungrily awaiting more images and information, but like a computer it is forced into another mode. Yet the little white discs with a dent down the middle are no panacea; whenever I take one of these thought guillotines I feel trapped in a grey zone, see-sawing between mid- and shallow slumber, mind and body dulled but not of their own accord. I sleep, but it is nearly always a vacant, songless sleep, as if I were even more distanced than usual from the apparatus that generates dreams.

*

It was in early 2003 when I moved to Berlin, a city dense with its own spectres, that my insomnia intensified. Night felt stranger, more enigmatic, so laden with signals it was hard ever to fully shut out. My senses were aware of some kind of continuum existing between the material world and the imaginary, the fantastical and the banal. Loping shadows, lights buzzing at empty tram shelters, a gauzy sheet flapping over giant scaffolding: the possibilities of projection were infinite. Close your eyes and you'd miss them.

At home in my fourth-floor flat in Prenzlauer Berg, night held a dreamy and tranquil stillness, a silence that remained for the most part undefiled by disembodied voices and the distant murmur of traffic. From my window I'd gaze out at the moon gently rocking over the court-yard, the silhouettes of trees, the darkened windows of my neighbours, and feel part of a greater act of contempla-tion. I sensed that if ever my night were to turn mystical, it would happen there.

Even the paintings in museums seemed to contain a more penetrating night, especially at the Alte Nationalgal-erie, where I would return again and again to the room of Caspar David Friedrichs and fantasise about entering every moonlit landscape. The figures in these paintings all have their backs to the viewer, a reminder of how pri-vate and solitary those hours ultimately are, regardless of whether one is accompanied.

Sometimes I would venture out into the city's other am-bit, the one galvanised by dusk and driven by a much more frenzied tempo. Berlin is famously paradise for night owls of the social variety too, and there was never any shortage of activity. I could meet friends for a drink at midnight, see a band play at one, head somewhere else at three. Introspection had no place there; night meant action and camaraderie, a lively negation of its quieter impulses.

Yet whether I stayed home or ventured into the city, my sleep remained shallow, broken and hard-won.

There's a term in German, Kopfkino, which means the imagination left to run wild, often magnifying the disturbing, unpleasant thoughts best kept at the mind's edge. The image offered by its literal translation, 'mental cinema', is what I envision takes place each time I lay my head on the pillow: the projector switches on and the reel starts its endless loops, a whirring machine that comes alive just as I feel ready to shut down.

More and more, I began to feel the negative effects of insomnia. At night the contemplative moments receded, drowned out by the constant inner din. And by day it became harder to function – mood, memory and concentration under an unshakeable pall – and I often experienced vertigo as I walked down the street. The lifeless detachment I'd sunk into only seemed to mock the hours of oblivion for which I longed.

In this mood, I went to see my local doctor, discussed the issue with numerous friends. More than one person mentioned the sleep clinic at Charité, the esteemed university hospital in Mitte, so after a series of especially vexing nights I took an afternoon off work and headed over.

On the tram journey I began to feel calm, telling myself that rest would soon be within reach, that I was going to hand my nights over to someone else, let them solve the problem.

Once I arrived at the sprawling hospital complex I

followed the signs reading 'Schlaflabor' that led away from the sound and movement of the street and into Charité's great clinical silence of red brick. At reception a laconic woman handed me a form requesting basic details. After I'd filled it in, she showed me to an anteroom and asked me to take a seat.

Like the fraternity of smokers, there's a fraternity of insomniacs, the disquiet betrayed by dark crescents under the eyes, pale faces exposed to too much moonlight, or something altogether less visible yet somehow perceptible to fellow sufferers, a kind of low, tired crackle beneath the surface.

Yet here I encountered a less romantic version. Around me sat bleary-eyed mostly middle-aged men and women, nearly all of whom were nodding off in their chairs. Some were alone, others with an attentive spouse on whose shoulder they rested their heads. I found a seat, pulled out the book I'd brought with me and tried to read. A mobile phone rang in someone's pocket; its owner, asleep, didn't react. Someone nearby shifted. Someone else sighed. At one point a man arrived with a small suitcase, presumably to spend the night, and was quickly shown into a side room.

The entire time I sat there, not once did I see anyone look anyone else in the eye; we were like souls in purgatory who, despite enduring the same torment, preferred not to associate with one another.

Finally, after two hours during which I read most of the book I'd brought with me, every now and then glancing up to check on the others, came my turn.

A door opened and a stocky man in a white coat appeared and held out a hand, introducing himself as Dr.

Blau. I followed him into his office, bare apart from a cat calendar on the wall, and took a seat across from him. First a few questions, he said, and then we could discuss options.

How long had I suffered from insomnia, he wanted to know.

Since birth, I answered, which was more or less true.

He then inquired whether my problem was falling asleep, staying asleep or nightly wakings up. And whether I ground my teeth, napped during the day, took exercise regularly or smoked.

After a ten-minute litany of questions, during which I felt increasingly impatient and unsettled, Dr. Blau informed me that the cost of a three-night stay at the sleep clinic would be in the region of two thousand euros – yet a few openings remained for a free trial they were conducting the following week. I could sign up. He suggested a night. I accepted. He added my name to a list and asked me to return to the clinic by six p.m. on the agreed day and to bring a few garments and whatever else I might need.

In the anteroom, no one glanced up when I walked past.

As the tram glided through the city's dusk, past the bold glow of shop fronts and cafés, I reflected on how much insomnia had informed my work, both my fiction and more academic ventures – and on how much night had, in general, seeped into nearly everything I'd written.

I thought back to one of my earliest forays into fiction, written in my early twenties, a series of loosely strung vignettes entitled 'Memoirs of an Insomniac.' I can no longer find the manuscript, nor open the files on my computer, written in a programme now obsolete, but this is probably for the best. Yet I remember how necessary it had felt at the time, my first attempt at addressing whatever it was that had me in its grip.

I then thought about the stories I'd written so far in Berlin, some eventually published. My first piece had been about a Museum of Night housing, among its exhibits, a terrarium filled with enormous black flowers whose petals turned into moths (Nachtfalter, 'nightfolder'); a Nocturnograph, a device for measuring night; and an installation by Hamburg and Humbug Holograms & Dioramas Ltd. called City of Dreadful Night: A Victorian Night Walk as Experienced in Nineteenth-Century London, inspired by James Thomson's haunting poem. All were like materialisations of the nocturnal energy that seemed to inhabit me so strongly.

By the time the tram neared my stop, the shadows of dusk had deepened and consolidated and I realised how pervasive a theme both night and insomnia had been over the years, the immediate tropism I'd feel, whenever I sat down at my desk, towards the nocturnal. And though I've probably worked through at least some of it by now, to this day I cannot imagine ever having a central character who is a good sleeper, who misses out on the godless hours and is unfamiliar with that very particular current of despair.

And I too am so used to the script I cannot imagine it any other way. The thought of approaching bed with a sense of calm and genuine fatigue seems tantalisingly foreign.

That evening after my visit to Charité I began writing 'In the Arms of Morpheus', a story about a young woman who spends the night at a sleep clinic with disappointing results, and in the process I finished convincing myself that a session there would somehow be detrimental. The following morning, despite not having slept well, I rang the clinic and cancelled my appointment.

I remember a Hungarian writer friend being astonished when I told him I had never found myself entirely alone in a forest – how could one fully become a writer, or any kind of thinker, without this experience, he seemed to suggest, for this represented the ultimate confrontation with the self – and I suppose I feel similarly about insomnia.

The friendship between Goethe and Friedrich apparently suffered when Goethe asked Friedrich whether he would help him in the classification of clouds. Friedrich promptly answered no, explaining that this would signify the death of landscape.

For me, likewise, night would be disenchanted by the scientific explanation of phenomena that may instead be felt as magical, mystical or simply mysterious. And I can't help thinking, finally, of Kafka's aphorism 'A cage went in search of a bird'. Free up a space in the mind and another obsession will come to occupy it.

We are, to a large extent, our own jail keepers. Our conditions define us, add contours, accents, drama to our lives. And the longer they accompany us, our so-called afflictions, the more years we spend together, the harder it is to part ways.

The Allure of the Analogue

The magic lantern may seem like a prosaic object: a tin or wooden box fitted with a chimney, a set of lenses and a light source. But for nearly four centuries it has animated the walls of homes and theatres, first as a device for conjuring demons and later as a form of popular entertainment. It also served a social and didactic function, caught up in the eighteenth-century love of philosophical toys. Art historians used magic lanterns to illustrate their lectures, the temperance movement cast images of ruined lives and despair. Their projections could draw attention to details in paintings but also to harsh social realities.

The instrument is thought to have been invented around 1650 by the Dutch polymath Christiaan Huygens, to whom we also owe the pendulum clock and the discovery of the true shape of the rings of Saturn. Slides are inserted upside down, so that the image projects right side up, and the lantern is positioned at a distance from the screen determined by its lenses. Originally the images were miniatures, hand-painted on glass, but from the 1850s photographic slides began to dominate the market. Before a show, the room must be checked for light spills; full darkness is required for the lantern to work, since even a sliver of light will dilute the projection.

Many of the earliest lanterns were made in Germany in the workshops of the Nuremberg toy makers. 'Nürnberger Hand geht durch alle Land', went a popular fifteenth-century saying. Early allusions to projection devices can be found in Giovanni Fontana (c. 1420) and Giovanni della Porta (1589), but the first printed description appears in the second edition of *Ars magna lucis et umbrae* (1671) by Athanasius Kircher, a German Jesuit priest with prodigious curiosity, scientific prowess and imagination. Five years earlier, in August 1666, Samuel Pepys wrote in his diary about a man who brought him 'a lanthorn, with pictures in glasse, to make strange things appear on a wall, very pretty.' A few centuries later, Charles Dickens put on shows for his children and called London itself his magic lantern. It 'sets me up and starts me,' he wrote to John Forster. In *Remembrance of Things Past*, Proust's narrator projects toy lantern images into the dark of his bedroom, uncertain where his self ends and the sorcery begins.

The lanternist has both a physical and metaphorical relationship to space.

Illuminants evolved over the centuries: candle, Argand lamp, limelight, arc light, incandescent light bulbs, light-emitting diodes. The simplest shows used a single lantern. More sophisticated arrangements, better for spectacles, had two projectors side by side or stacked one above the other. Triunials, or three-tiered lanterns, created the most elaborate effects but were more expensive and harder to master. The most popular special effect, possible only with two or three lenses, was that of dissolving views, in which one landscape faded into another, or day transitioned into night. This technique also made use of an early version of the thought balloon, with an inset hovering above the subject: a girl asleep in a forest dreaming of witches flying overhead, a soldier of returning home. Other effects were produced by moving cranks, levers and handles. Slipping slides allowed for movement back and forth – eyes glancing left and right, rapid transformations. Lever slides created an arc, rotating handles a full circle.

In some cases, the lanternists themselves became part of the lore; the Savoyards, eighteenth-century humble wanderers, would leave their mountain homes in late October to travel the countryside with a magic lantern strapped to their backs, its tall chimney like a ship's funnel powering their journey. They led a portfolio existence, putting on peep shows by day and magic lantern shows by night, as well as offering their services as chimney sweeps. To judge from surviving engravings, Savoyards often played the hurdy-gurdy and kept as a companion a marmot, a large ground squirrel whose piercing squeaks must have added to the atmosphere. Savoyard lanterns, rough-and-ready objects that bore the marks of weather and regular use, tended to be crudely made and weak in illumination.

For two years, I was writer in residence at the Swedenborg Society, which has hundreds of lantern slides in its archive. As the culmination of my residency, the director, Stephen McNeilly, aware of my longstanding fascination with magic lanterns, invited me to put on a show, and create new stories around the images in the collection. The society, founded in 1810, is devoted to the study of the great eighteenth-century Swedish mystic Emanuel Swedenborg, who was also an illustrious scientist and inventor. He dreamt up water pumps and sluices, a flying machine and a submarine, and at the age of twenty-eight was appointed General Assessor of Mines by the King of Sweden. A spiritual awakening in his mid-fifties led him to spend the rest of his life contemplating the ways in which matter related to spirit.

The relationship between the material and the immaterial is what animates the magic lantern, bridging the apparent divide between the rationalist impulses of Enlightenment thought and the mystical. Although the slides in the collection were made long after Swedenborg's death in 1772, his taxonomical impulse and his investigations into the afterlife make him the ideal tutelary presence for a magic lantern show, and the oak-panelled neoclassical hall at Swedenborg House seemed an ideal venue.

The Society has two lanterns of its own but we decided to contact Jeremy Brooker, then Chairman of the Magic Lantern Society, who along with wife, Carolyn, has been putting on magic lantern shows for decades. I took the train to Canterbury and in his cave-like study, the walls hung with dangling skeletons and unusual musical instruments – Jeremy is also a professional musician – we exchanged early ideas. We wanted to offer audiences the full spectacle, to show the different registers the instrument can produce, and so we decided to include some of Jeremy's slides too, as preludes to my stories. This meant we could show hand-painted slides as well as photographic ones, offsetting contemplative moods with moments of joviality. Many of Jeremy's slides are playful and nimble, while those from the Swedenborg collection, largely monochrome, emanate an otherworldly stillness.

The Swedenborg slides feature landscapes, street scenes

and scientific diagrams used to accompany lectures. There was also a box labelled 'Portraits and Busts', with dozens of images of former members of the Society, a procession of eloquent faces, male and female. Scholars have struggled to learn more about their origins. It is not known when most of the photographs were taken, nor when the slides were made, nor by whom. James Wilson, an editor and librarian at the Society, recently discovered that the majority of the slides were acquired in 1910 and 1912 by two men from the New Church: the Reverend J.R. Rendell and Alfred Henry Stroh. Rendell had a keen interest in photography; Stroh was an eminent theologian. The only box that can be dated is labeled: 'Seventy-five Slides, illustrating a

Visit to Skandinavia, LECTURE delivered by Dr Freda Griffith, 1952.' Griffith was the Society's secretary for more than three decades and devoted much of her energy to producing a third Latin edition of Swedenborg's eight-volume *Arcana Coelestia* (1749). It's revealing to see what her eye landed on during her travels: libraries, bridges, ships in the harbour. Most of the photographs contain no people, as though taken during a lull in humanity.

The three-and-a-quarter-inch square glass plates were kept in tight rows and had funerary black tape around their edges. Day after day in the top-floor library of the Society, presided over by a marble bust of Swedenborg and hundreds of translated volumes of his work, I sifted through the slides and laid out those I found most evocative – the silhouette of a hatted man under a bridge, vacant rooms with ghostly furniture, a tree-lined avenue with an overturned bicycle. I lifted them out of their sarcophagal boxes, the string holding them closed crumbling to the touch, held them up to the overhead light or placed them on a makeshift light box. The longer I spent with the slides, the greater the urge to both preserve and articulate their mystery. After a few days, as if in a séance, fully formed beats began to enter my head, and from these phrases emerged whole sequences, constellations that insisted on existing together even though the images came from different series. I surrendered to a state of free association and felt an exhilarating sense of compression and distillation as stories grew out of unlikely juxtapositions.

Jeremy and I had decided our themes would encompass the passage of time, ghosts and the supernatural, travel (physical and metaphorical) and the natural world (fantastical creatures and natural phenomena). I titled our spectacle 'Stilled Shadows', although the more I prepared, the more I thought about the movement that awaited the stillness. A slide is usually projected for around ten seconds, so a five-minute story requires around thirty slides. Different sections call for a faster or slower rhythm; in the right context, an image might linger for thirty seconds or more, especially when accompanied by expansive music. Our show lasted for an hour and used more than a hundred slides.

The first performance took place on 21 October 2021. Until that evening, I hadn't seen any of the slides projected. As I looked up from my text at the images, new details came into view – objects in a room, a face in a parked car. The show was accompanied by the silent film pianist Costas Fotopoulos, but this wasn't the only sound the audience was attuned to: people later commented on the clacking of the slides, or rather, of the wooden carriers into which the slides fitted, as Jeremy would insert one straight after Carolyn had removed the preceding, a complicated choreography in the dark that required tremendous concentration. Seamless timing is essential to avoid the dreaded empty circle of light. This is part of the allure of the analogue: it's impossible to forget the human behind the illusion. In our show, the magic lantern occupies a table at the centre of the room, flanked on either side by rows of spectators, with the mechanism in full view. Rather than detracting from the experience, the exposed machinery adds to the sense of enchantment.

There's something inherently ghostly about the magic lantern but its most overtly macabre manifestation was the spectacle of phantasmagoria, fashionable in the late eighteenth and early nineteenth century. Ghoulish figures were cast onto a translucent screen or a cloud of smoke with the help of a fantascope, a lantern on wheels that could zoom in and out, allowing the phantoms to grow in size as if rushing towards the audience. These shows were accompanied by the strains of a glass harmonica and clanking chains, thunder, church bells. The lantern would be concealed, the source of projection a mystery. The most celebrated phantasmagorist was the Belgian showman Étienne-Gaspard Robertson, who installed himself in the Capuchin Convent in Paris after the French Revolution, resurrecting traumas not yet laid to rest.

The ghosts in our magic lantern show are quieter. They haunt their spaces unobtrusively, exude a spectral melancholy. They invite us to make psychological readings of inanimate objects. Among my stories is one about a reclusive writer who leaves home to search for her missing cat, and wanders through her past as she roams the city. Another woman, feeling captive to the fine flat she has inherited, begins to perceive an unsettling presence in a marble-topped table. A slide with the handwritten words 'The Mechanism and Substance of Mind', the title of a lecture on Swedenborgian theory, leads to a vignette about a young woman who is prey to a deepening solitude. A slide showing a pair of old-fashioned Swedish phone boxes, one for local calls, one for long distance, inspires a dialogue, each phone box given its own musical identity. As the stories unfold, the focus moves from individual portraits to a wider vision of the cosmos.

Today, the magic lantern is kept alive by the UK's Magic Lantern Society, which hosts regular meetings, provides online resources and publishes a quarterly journal listing forthcoming shows, exhibitions, restoration tips, advice sought on strange acquisitions, and sightings of lanterns in recent films or TV programmes. Many of the personal ads are performances in themselves: 'Young(ish) female member, five foot one, seeks Magic Lantern chimney maker to create stunning new chimney for wooden lantern. Current tea-towel chimney substitute lets out light and is becoming singed'; 'For sale: Hand-painted double slipper slide: acrobat arches himself for vertical take-off, he succeeds only to tip over and land on his face. Excellent condition. £30.'

My modest collection of slides includes a painted portrait of the sun, captured by a stranger on a summer's day long ago. I bought it last year during a meeting of the Society (at the back of the room, tables were set up with items for sale or barter). The sun is surrounded by an orange halo, billowy purple clouds and a sky in different shades of blue. I like imagining it was painted by William Blake. The sun's centre is transparent, allowing it to take on the colour of whatever background it is set against. Along the bottom of the frame is written in black ink: 'The Sun as on July 30th, 1817.' If you look closely you can see four sunspots, and perhaps something more, impossible to read with the naked eye. I have yet to see it projected.

Hymn to the Stray Dog

Here it comes, its gait bold and determined or else hesitant and subdued, depending on its experience in the world thus far. Here it is, making its way towards us, dodging cars, hugging walls, sniffing out the situation, on the lookout for voices or gestures that may grant some insight into a temperament. The stray dog. It must gauge what the human intends before coming any closer, whether he or she intends kindness or cruelty. It isn't aware of the social contract between us, but I am, and I shall honour it as best I can, despite concerns about startling it away or frightening it into defensive mode. It takes a few steps forward, devours my offering and vanishes back into the labyrinth of Mexico City.

In London one rarely sees stray dogs. Not long ago, a Mexican friend who lives here too commented on how she misses seeing stray dogs in the background. This city feels somewhat empty without them, she said, like there's something missing from the panorama. I remember being struck by her words and dwelling on them for a long while afterwards. If anything, I was thankful for their absence. Not because I don't love dogs – I certainly do – but because ever since childhood the sight of a stray has nearly always triggered despair: where did it come from, where was it going, always hungry, always on the move. On family car trips I couldn't avert my eyes quickly enough from the road: the sight of one run-over would haunt me for days. Yet I now began to think about how despite their precarious situation, so unresolved, they represent an indomitable spirit, and in this aspect too they are emblematic of our country.

Over the centuries, dogs have been an enduring feature of Mexican life and art. Long before the Spanish conquistadors arrived in the New World with their snarling wolfhounds and mastiffs, the breed most familiar to the Aztecs was the hairless black Xoloitzcuintli, or Xolo for short. In life it was a companion and foodstuff (indeed, a delicacy for the nobles), and often used to warm a cold bed at night. In death the Xolo was considered to be a guide through the underworld and would carry the soul of its deceased owner in its mouth. Yet the Spaniards who sailed over in the late 1510s and early 1520s used their hounds as weapons of war, and transformed the dog from ally into adversary, a feared animal that would often tear its victims to pieces. Once the Conquest was largely complete and the dogs' job for the most part done, they were said to hungrily roam the streets in search of prey, thus becoming, perhaps, the earliest incarnations of strays in Mexico. Since those times the dog has returned to being a creature man can easily subjugate, but somewhere within its scrawny figure resides a phantom of that battle.

When I handed in my latest novel, *Sea Monsters*, my editors commented with some surprise on the number of mentions of dogs in my book: thirty-seven. But they are a *leitmotif* of daily life, I explained, present in nearly every landscape and cityscape, a mobile part of the composition.

I describe the local dogs in Mexico City, where my narrator lives, both those who have owners and those who inhabit the collapsed ruins left by the 19 September 1985 earthquake: *a menagerie of strays, spectral cats with faint meows and mangy dogs who'd spend hours pawing at imaginary food in the crevices.* I was also intent on depicting the beach dogs, one of the most memorable features of my trip to Oaxaca: *The dogs in Zipolite may have been safe from city woes, yet all day long they wandered up and down the beach as if scavenging for something not provided by the landscape.* In both cases these dogs evoke a sense of disquiet, a search for something beyond the here and now, and my adolescent narrator feels similarly restless and unfulfilled, although in her case she has a secure home and parents who look after her (if anything, she is after a less secure scenario that throws open the possibility of change).

I wanted stray dogs to feature in my novel as a hymn to my country, to survival, and of course to the animals themselves. Yet looking back, on a more figurative level I also wanted them to exist as a kind of antidote to plot expectation (though what cultivated reader reads solely for 'plot'?). Stray dogs proceed – seemingly – with only a vague sense of purpose; their presence creates a mood, feeds into an atmosphere, without signposting a major development. They may suggest movement, and appetite and desire, but they don't impose action on a scene, they just *are* – and what is so wrong with that? Real life tends to be composed of quiet moments that fill the years between a handful of defining ones. A writer can choose to represent these quieter moments instead. A writer can favour meandering narratives – stray dog narrations, one could call them – driven by something more subtle and inscrutable than 'action'. Movement within a novel takes place, after all, on many levels.

*

Dogs were an important symbol for me while writing the book, but they also represent a real concern. Mexico currently has more stray dogs than any other country in Latin America and the number is rising steadily. In recognition of their plight, a charity called Milagros Caninos erected the Monument to the Stray Dog at the side of an unfrequented road in the south-lying borough of Tlalpan in 2008. Most monuments in Mexico tend to be of heroic individuals empowered by battle, yet this subject is skinny and forlorn with a low-hanging head and jutting ribs, its body hunched over in defeat. The only battle it has won is that of narrow survival. Every now and then a scribble of graffiti appears on its metal flanks, gradually washed off by the rain. On the base there was at first a plaque that read: 'My only crime was to be born and have lived on the streets, or to have been abandoned. I didn't ask for this, and despite the blows and indifference the only thing I demand is whatever remains of your love. I don't want to suffer, surviving in this world is a matter of horror. Help me, please!' A stray dog that has been given a name has a far greater chance of survival, Hannah Arendt famously remarked. Unlike other strays, this imaginary dog was granted a name, Peluso, but even that failed to rescue him from oblivion. Last year the plaque was stolen, deemed more valuable as scrap metal probably, and the statue is currently in a sorry state.

I can't help but wonder whether the mere fact of the monument's existence, an existence minimised by its remote location and persistent neglect, captures Mexicans' ambivalence towards this canine that has accompanied them over the centuries. During their peripatetic lives stray dogs are subject to the capricious behaviour of humans, on the receiving end of kindness, cruelty and indifference. (Every December, for instance, hundreds are left behind by pilgrims at the Basilica of Guadalupe; the pilgrims feed them along the way, acquiring a companion for their travels, but after paying their respects to the Virgin, compassion is shed and they jump on a bus and abandon them.)

A staggering seventy per cent of dogs in Mexico have no real home. Solitary or in packs, they occupy the lowest rank, along with stray cats, of any urban or rural hierarchy. My sister and I would often feed the scrawny mongrels that wandered the unpaved streets of Contepec, Michoacán, the village where my father grew up, dogs he describes in *The Child Poet* as the colour of the sun, of a yellow that seemed sprouted from the fields: 'They would attach themselves to the first person who walked by, and for a while had an owner, until a door closed in their face and they'd go back to being no one's dog.' We too were sometimes guilty of deserting an animal at the door; our grandmother already had her menagerie of cats, birds and dogs and we weren't allowed to add to it.

Shadowing our steps or pursuing paths of their own, stray dogs lead a parallel existence to ours, and in cities seem to gravitate towards other beings who dwell in the liminal spaces of society. When my sister filmed her documentary *Children of the Street*, she was keen to depict the Mexican street children's symbiotic relationship with the

149

dogs who accompanied them day and night, sharing in their fortunes and misfortunes (speeding cars, predatory humans) – each a mirror of the other's vulnerability but also a source of comfort and friendship.

In Juan Rulfo's rural dramas, the barking of dogs acquires a spectral reality, largely ancestral, announcing a reckoning to come. Malcolm Lowry's *Under the Volcano* concludes with the image of the tormented consul's corpse thrown into a ditch, a dead 'pariah dog' tossed in after him. More recently, the Belgian/Mexican artist Francis Alÿs made a video called *El Gringo*, in which a patchwork of mongrels on a dust road gather round the camera in an ascending chorus, their vigorous barks an almost comedic expression of territoriality. Here there is little doubt as to who belongs and who is intruding, though the different angles from which the video is shot suggest there is more than one dimension to the conflict.

Even more than the long-suffering donkey, which in recent decades has all but vanished from the Mexican countryside, the stray dog endures yet rarely forms part of the action. Always present, always in limbo, its uncertain gait identifiable from afar, it shares our public spaces, infusing them with a noble life force, its own existence endangered yet its kind never in danger of extinction.

Baroque

Each time I return to Mexico I find myself marvelling at how many elements of daily life there could, in some way, be described as Baroque: our sunsets, our cuisine, our pollution, our corruption. Century after century, the country has exhibited a great tendency towards exuberance, and a natural bent for the strange and the marvellous. There's a constant play between veiling and unveiling (even in our newscasts, one senses indirect meaning in everything), as well as a fluidity of form, in which excess triumphs, every time, over restraint.

Three hundred years of colonial rule produced an intense syncretism of indigenous and European cultures, a bold new aesthetic accompanied by many new paradoxes, and these can be glimpsed today in both lighter and darker manifestations, some playful and others barbaric.

Mexican Baroque emerged from the conquest of the New World, from the long, fraught process of negotiation and subjugation that began to unfold once the Spaniards established their rule in 1521. The European monarchs wanted as much gold as their conquistadors could plunder, while their missionaries sought to convert the pagan savages to Catholicism. The Aztecs of course had their own gods, a monumental pantheon that included the fierce and formidable Quetzalcoatl and Huitzilopochtli, yet these ancient powers proved no match for colonial rapacity.

There was one pivotal overlap between the two religions, however, a fortuitous convergence which helped ease the transition from the Aztec cosmology to the Catholic faith. And this was the 'theatre of death' present in both religions. Accustomed to their own culture of human sacrifice, the Indians identified with the Crucifixion and other violent chapters in the new theology, and were thus gradually lured by its passions and taste for the macabre. In artistic portrayals of certain scenes from the New Testament, the blood and drama were laid on thick.

The Churrigueresque style brought over from Spain, a highly florid and heavily laden version of Rococo, found its most triumphant expression, one could argue, in Mexico. The church architects were Spanish, yet the artisans and labourers were indigenous and mestizo, and these asserted their autonomy from the metropolis by adding local materials such as tezontle, a red porous volcanic stone, and local motifs, with quetzals and hummingbirds and faces with native features finding their way into the chiselled landscapes. In all their magnificence, the gilt altars and church facades also betrayed a horror of silence and empty space, every inch of wood, stucco and stone teeming with detail, as if replicating the delirious splendour of the natural world beyond.

Despite the number of masterly creations that resulted, Mexican Baroque mostly emerged from a clash of cultures, from antagonism rather than harmony, and this is largely what grants it its dynamic force. Its art rejected straight lines and predictable paths, revelling in a liberated geometry that mirrored the new unstable and multi-caste society that had risen from the embers. The monolithic sculptures of the Aztecs and earlier pre-Hispanic civilisations – signs of a certain stability – were replaced by a more fluid and volatile art, one which favoured movement over form, agility over monumentality.

Like most art of the Baroque, it too thrived off a play of contrasts and opposites, and this was most poignantly articulated in the historical counterpoint between the Aztec emperor Moctezuma and the Spanish conquistador Hernán Cortés, the dialectic between victor and vanquished spilling over into one between old gods and new, the awe of the conquistadors upon discovering this marvel of a land versus the increasing disenchantment of its natives, their gods toppled, their beliefs exploited. To a large extent, the soul of modern Mexico was born from this collision.

One arena in present-day Mexico in which a conflict of archetypes can be witnessed literally is in the spectacle of *lucha libre*, or free-style wrestling, another European import to which was added local colour and verve. Different theories exist regarding its origins: some say an early variant was brought over in 1863 during the French intervention, or in 1910 by a Spanish boxing promoter; a more accepted notion is that the sport came to Mexico in the early 1920s courtesy of two duelling Italian theatre troupes.

Everything about the performance favours emotion over form. The movements are exaggerated, as are the wrestlers themselves, massive hulks of men in tights who wear capes like those of superheroes and shiny carnivalesque masks that hide their faces. There's a certain splendour to them, but once the match begins the splendour is undercut by an atmosphere of buffoonery. At rest, the wrestlers appear regal and imposing. In motion, the elegance is quickly undermined by their comical leaps and bounds. It is as if they start off by embodying the first period of Baroque in Mexico, in the late seventeenth century, characterised by solemn church facades, rich and refined, and then they go on to embody its second period, from the mid-eighteenth century, which was more opulent and chaotic, an architecture of Solomonic columns that twist, spiral and writhe.

The wrestlers' masks often evoke their powers and persona: El Santo, Blue Demon, Fray Tormenta, Huracán Ramírez, Rey Misterio. They are costumed heroes and villains, engaged in a jocular battle between good and evil. The Baroque fondness for extremes is felt in every match, which is fought between a *técnico* – one who follows the rules and plays cleanly and gracefully – and a *rudo* – one who transgresses, breaking codes with relish. In this play of adversaries, there is no guarantee that good will win. In fact, the *rudos* are often expected to triumph, hinting at a cultural acceptance that righteousness, in Mexico at least, isn't necessarily rewarded.

In a sense, the showdown between Moctezuma and Cortés could similarly be envisioned as a battle between a *técnico* and a *rudo*; the Aztec emperor, honest and honourable and deferential to his guests, played by the rules, while the conquistador lied and cheated and, thanks in part to his deviousness, succeeded in bringing down an entire civilisation.

The wild gestures that fuel the *lucha libre* spectacle elicit a frantic emotional intensity. Audiences work themselves into a lather, subjecting the wrestlers to a loud repertoire of insults, mostly bawdy and vulgar, as if they were taking sides in some kind of moral contest rather than a sporting tournament.

In Baroque art movement tends to be centrifugal, a restlessness away from the centre, as opposed to the Classical impulse of restraint. Although the wrestlers lunge at one another, they are constantly being cast outwards, either by their opponent's thrust or the elastic ring, their main instrument for propulsion. Performers often take flying leaps outside the ring and land in the audience. Similar to what Caravaggio did in his paintings, these 'suicides', as the moves are called, break down the boundary and remove the safety barrier between viewer and spectacle; one can smell the sweat, feel the flesh, hear the grunts, almost grasp the energy of the wrestler as he comes crashing into us.

Even the geometry of the ring is defied, its quadrangle stretched and deformed again and again. The rapid shifting of planes – between floor and air, the ring and beyond – is forged by grand aerial manoeuvres and gestures of torsion and contortion. Every effort is answered with a counter-effort, every movement turned into its opposite, a great elasticity between up and down as each man tries to bring his opponent to the ground. In this endless curling and coiling, transcendence is, at least corporeally, denied.

Something deeply Dionysian haunts the spectacle, chaotic and unpolished. And yet it is often marked by pathos – sometimes the mere sight of a massive lump of a man unable to haul himself up or, even more so, when a wrestler is defeated and his mask removed. The moment his identity is revealed, his strength and aura dissolve.

A more recent and dismaying phenomenon of Baroque excess and hyperbole, where the human body again becomes the site of transformation yet the spectacle of bloodshed is real, not staged, is within the violence wrought by the warring drug cartels.

Since 2006, Mexico has been in the grip of a disastrous war on drugs, initiated by our then president Felipe Calderón when he took office. Over sixty thousand individuals have lost their lives as the cartels battle among themselves for territory while a weakened military and often corrupt police force try desperately to control them. Nearly every day the news offers reports of beheadings and dismemberment, of a violence and brutality so extreme that even the depiction of severed body parts in Goya's *Disasters of War* seems restrained. The deep-rooted anxiety about fragmentation in Goya and also Bosch's work is surpassed by the chilling real-life images of human mutilation we have in Mexico. It goes without saying that narco-violence is not an art, yet the graphic *mise-en-scènes* could similarly be read as allegories of great socio-political disintegration, and the headless bodies as metaphors for a country without any real leadership.

Mexicans are accustomed to severed body parts; they have been an element in our landscape since pre-Hispanic times. Skulls in particular feature in every one of our civilisations, the hollow eye sockets and bared teeth a presence from ancient eras through to modern. Yet these skulls have become so detached from their cadavers they seem to exist entirely on their own, devoid of humanity. And it is one thing to see images in stone at the Museum of Anthropology and quite another to witness heads with their hair and flesh still on them, faces one could have glimpsed on the metro yesterday. The ancient skulls formed part of a metaphysics, whereas the decapitated heads of today signal chaos and collapse.

In Uruapán, a city in my father's north-western state of Michoacán, masked men stormed into a discotheque called Sol y Sombra (Sun and Shadow) and tossed five severed heads onto the dance floor. This incident, which took place over ten years ago, was one of the first outings of La Familia, a drug cartel composed of right-wing vigilantes who quickly established their bloody reign over the region. The photographic image of these decapitated heads, each with its trail of blood where it has rolled out from the black plastic bag, is hard to erase from memory. Their eyes are closed, their faces a shiny olive colour; the gangrene of death has yet to set in. In their midst, a large scroll emblazoned with a warning for rival cartels, a hand-written message that ends with the words 'Divine Justice'.

Other cartels, like the Zetas, the Gulf Cartel and the Sinaloa Cartel, are similarly fond of leaving behind gruesome *memento mori*. Bodies, often headless, are dangled from bridges or left in segments by the side of the road. Here Baroque is taken to an extreme, deformed into excess and true monstrosity. The tremendous striving for effect, a desire to make the most startling impact on the senses, has mutated into an unabashed theatricality of the utmost violence.

There are, these days, few signs of redemption. In a regrettable twist on the Baroque, its original vitality has been contorted, redirected towards death rather than life. One finds similar aesthetic criteria, a similar dynamism and instinct for theatricality, yet the early religious impulses have morphed into their opposite. And for some the only religion left, it seems, is death itself.

Perhaps the most literal manifestation of contemporary Baroque – a true syncretism of Spanish Catholicism and pre-Hispanic beliefs – is to be found in the cult of La Santa Muerte, or Holy Death, the patron saint of the Mexican underworld, who is a sanctified personification of death herself. Though her cult incorporates dozens of Catholic rituals, she remains vehemently unrecognised by the church.

The millions who worship La Santa Muerte tend to belong to the more marginalized or endangered strata of society: criminals, transsexuals, drug dealers, prostitutes, taxi drivers, police officers. They are individuals who live by violence or are threatened by it, those who exist in a perpetual twilight and, professionally, mostly by night. And they come to her for protection.

I first encountered La Santa Muerte at her main altar in Tepito, Mexico City's shadowy sanctum of drugs and contraband. There she stood, behind a glass pane, a tall skeleton in a long black wig, a jewelled crown, a sparkling gold dress and a diaphanous cape. She was heavily adorned, an embodiment of Baroque's dual pull towards death and sensuality, and I couldn't help feeling like I was seeing a pre-Hispanic skull in Spanish robes. In one hand she held a globe of the world, in the other the scales of justice. Spread out at her feet was a semi-circle of figurines, smaller versions of herself, and a flickering landscape of ephemeral offerings: candles, apples, flowers, incense, beer, bottles of tequila, lit cigarettes. I watched as the devotees queued up to press their hands against the pane and murmur their prayers, then quietly deposit a gift.

When the Spaniards arrived in Mexico, Moctezuma, believing they were gods, had his emissaries take Cortés tortillas smeared with human blood as an offering. The emperor himself was a sybaritic gourmet, presented with around three hundred dishes a day made from ingredients brought in from all over the country. Human sacrifice also formed part of the cuisine, and his priests would cook up the remains of sacrificial victims in squash flower soup. The most Baroque dish to emerge from the Conquest is mole poblano, a thick sauce like dark blood concocted from chocolate, almonds, spices and three types of chilli, originally put together by nuns in a convent in Puebla. In Mexico there's a saying that the spicier a food, and the more it makes you cry, the tastier it is. True culinary enjoyment should be accompanied by a bit of agony, and so it is that to this day mole remains our most beloved dish, a reminder of the turbulent forces from which modern Mexico was born.

15 Moments of Lightness in Fanny and Alexander

(May 2020)

It's hard to ignore the paradox we're currently living: our world brought to a standstill, daily life grounded to a halt by a virus that leaps about with an agility we're denied. The more the virus travels, the more we must stay in place, succumbing in more ways than one to the gravity of the moment. At the beginning of lockdown, I began thinking about works that featured characters who suffered some form of entrapment and found release through their imagination. Ingmar Bergman's *Fanny and Alexander* (1982), one of my favourite films since adolescence, soon rose to mind. Set in the Swedish town of Uppsala in the early twentieth century, it centres around the Ekdahl family and specifically sister and brother Fanny and Alexander, who live through a series of ever-darkening tribulations. It's not a film one would associate with lightness any more than Bergman's other work, yet in it I found many moments that captured a striving towards physical or existential weightlessness, a weightlessness that threw into question, or helped alleviate, the oppressive ground pull of reality.

1. Prologue. Alexander gazes into his toy paper theatre, his head resting on a hand. Nine little flames dance in the foreground. The puppets and cardboard backdrops lack material density and can easily be rearranged; nothing is immutable.

2. Alexander wanders the empty rooms of his grandmother's sumptuous apartment, calling out. No one replies. The clock chimes three, cherubs revolve on a pedestal. In a corner, the marble statue of a semi-nude woman is suddenly bathed in otherworldly light. She begins to move her arms to the ethereal tune of a music box.

3. The presence of his sister, Fanny. Blue-eyed and moon-faced, always in her flaxen braids and pinafore, she is imbued with a lightness that eludes her raven-haired brother. Despite living through the same traumas, she seems less haunted and moves gracefully through the film, a silent witness.

4. The presence of his luminous grandmother Helena Ekdahl, née Mandelbaum. The matriarch, a repository of wisdom. She tends to her family's suffering, listens to their woes in her light-filled conservatory.

5. Christmas revels. Dinner, followed by the extended family and servants dancing spiritedly through the rooms in single file. This is the only moment of total levity in the film, when earthly worries are shed.

6. The children are put to bed. Alexander's eye falls on a magic lantern beckoning from a table. He treats the other children to a show, casting a beam across the darkened room. A ghostly figure floats into the frame, an uncanny intrusion into the domestic space. Like the characters in the film, the lantern is poised between the solid traditions of the nineteenth century and the atomised sorcery of the twentieth.

7. Shortly after Christmas their father, a struggling theatre manager, collapses on stage while playing the ghost of Hamlet's father, and dies. The father becomes a ghost, one that will exist beyond any theatre or magic lantern show.

Then follows a chapter from which all forms of lightness are absent. Fanny and Alexander's mother, Emilie, marries Edvard Vergérus, the stern Lutheran bishop who presided over their father's funeral. The children move with her to his home and are put in a tower. Edvard insists they leave behind their books, toys and dolls. The rich palette shifts to heavy greys and black. Their imprisonment is further embodied in Elsa, the bishop's obese, toad-like aunt, who is mute and immobile. Edvard feels threatened by Alexander's flights of imagination, the one sphere over which he has no control, and beats him when he tells a lie. The only movement is that of the river below, flowing through the town, rushing and fugitive. Alexander gazes down at it through barred windows. Emilie has not found the spiritual lightness she desperately sought; she realises her grave error.

8. It is Uncle Isak Jacobi, the grandmother's lover, who rescues the children from the crushing weight of the bishop's

rule. He appears in a black hat and overcoat in a horse-pulled cart and says he has come to purchase a wooden chest. While Edvard goes to sign a paper Isak finds the children and has them remove their shoes and quickly crawl inside.

9. Suspecting a ruse, the bishop and his sister rush up to the nursery. In a moment of divine intervention – Isak implores the heavens – they see a simulacrum: Fanny and Alexander lie curled on the floor asleep, at the centre of the room. 'Don't touch them!' Emilie cries out.

10. Inspired by a Jewish antiques shop Bergman visited as a child, Isak's dimly lit home quivers with magic and possibility. Rows of puppets with carved faces hang from the ceiling, nodding as the children walk past. Unlit chandeliers emit a numinous tinkling. Isak lives with his two nephews, Aron the puppeteer and Ishmael, his brother, who is apparently mad and dangerous and must be kept in a locked room. Everything forms part of a mysterious ecosystem in a state of suspension, its residents endowed with a certain agility acquired through mystical thought.

That night, Alexander loses his way back to his bed after visiting the bathroom and has three significant encounters.

11. In a room full of crystal vessels and chandeliers, Alexander holds a conversation with his father's ghost. His father apologises for his powerlessness. In Hebrew the word for respect is *kavod*, which also means 'weight'; you impart weight to your parents in order to find your own lightness. Yet Alexander doesn't seem ready to do so.

12. Alexander then holds a conversation with God, who admonishes him from behind a door. The door opens and a giant marionette tumbles out. Aron leaps from behind. He reminds Alexander that nothing is what it seems. 'Uncle Isak says we are surrounded by realities, one outside the other.'

13. They hear a distant song. It is Ishmael, singing. Aron leads Alexander to his room. Ishmael is androgynous, seer-like and menacing. In his diary, published later in his autobiographical *Images: My Life in Film* (1994), Bergman described Ishmael as 'an idiot with the face of an angel, a thin, fragile body and colourless eyes that see all. He is able to do evil. He is like a membrane for wishes that quivers with the slightest touch.'

14. Ishmael can read Alexander's wishes. More important, he can set them in motion. He speaks softly, running his hands over Alexander's face and chest. The scene cuts to the bishop's home, where Elsa knocks over her bedside lamp and begins a fire. Writhing in flames, she bursts into the bishop's room and clutches him. 'The burning woman [annihilates] the bishop,' wrote Bergman, as if describing a concluding chess move.

15. Epilogue. Alexander nestles beside his grandmother. She reads to him from August Strindberg's *Dream Play* (1901): 'Time and space do not exist. Only a flimsy framework of reality. The Imagination spins, weaving new patterns.' The ticking of a clock. Alexander drifts off.

Bergman's mother was ill with Spanish influenza when he was born in 1918, and he was sickly as a child. That early existential dread courses through all of his work (most overtly in *The Seventh Seal* [1957], set in plague-ravished medieval Europe) and often there exists little to offset it. In *Fanny and Alexander* he emphasises the importance of creating one's little world within the larger one beyond, to escape into spaces where the stifling concreteness of reality temporarily dissolves, or at least wears a different face. At a time when so much of life feels petrified, it's easy to forget the vitalising function of lightness, in this case a lightness attained through reverie. And though our reverie may never be entirely free of gravity or menace, it grants us agility, a movement free of gravitational laws and limitations. We should allow ourselves to be borne aloft.

The Tension of
Transience

Did we feel safe at the time? I no longer remember. My father had read in a newspaper that El Nueve was dangerous, so whenever we went there, which was often, my sister and I would say we were going elsewhere.

At the age of seventeen, one drama swiftly supplanted the next, just as one obsession drove out another, yet I shall never forget the events of Friday, 19 April 1989. At first it seemed like simply another night out, another nocturnal reply to the daylight hours, yet two details had already set it apart. At school I'd received an admissions letter from Harvard: in other words, that autumn I would be leaving home, and Mexico, possibly forever. I also recall it was a full moon; there are at least twelve full moons a year and most of the time I wouldn't attribute much importance to them, but that night it felt as though the moon was exerting an unusual pull.

As was the custom, a male friend – in this case, Yoshua – came to pick us up. As was also the custom, my father saw us into the car, checking with Yoshua that he indeed intended to keep his promise and deliver us home by our curfew.

On some nights two thirty seemed generous; on others, cruelly early.

Located halfway down Calle Londres in downtown Zona Rosa, El Nueve had been opened in 1978 by the Frenchman Henri Donnadieu as an alternative to the more mainstream synthetic nightlife that dominated the city at the time. It was a place that championed tolerance and creativity, and a gay haven that hosted underground gigs, drag shows and magazine launches. Donnadieu envisioned night itself as a cultural enterprise in which everyone should take part, and its *noches bugas*, or straight nights, attracted younger folk like us, lured above all by the music: goth, post-punk and industrial. At the entrance beckoned the sign ELLAS NO PAGAN (women don't pay) and, even more enticingly, another sign, further in: BARRA LIBRE, free drinks all night, although it was widely believed that ether was added to the ice to curb the drinking.

Upon arriving that April night my sister and I encountered some of the regulars. There was Adán the Aviator, in his bomber jacket, goggles and motorcycle boots, aviator cap with earflaps; he always seemed about to lift off but in reality never left the dance floor. Standing against a wall wrapped in his melancholic aura was El Sauce Llorón, the weeping willow, a magazine editor by day and drama queen by night. Tall with a Roman nose, he was often in tears over insurmountable dramas, real and imagined, his long black hair framing his face like a shroud. There, too, were El Nueve's transvestites, presiding over the rooms like rare nocturnal flowers. And finally, Los Ultravox, a group of young men in grey raincoats. These were their night selves; I had no idea what most of them did during the day – some must've held down humdrum jobs, others may have been students – any further knowledge would have dented the enchantment.

The dance floor officially opened at midnight, announced by a clap of thunder and the appearance of the smoke machine. Each week it was the same: the DJ would put on *Carmina Burana* and the chanting would build in volume, like the re-enactment of something medieval, bombastic, portentous, that came rolling in from a distant century. After a few minutes, its dramaturgy would segue into the beats of the Sisters of Mercy's 'Lucretia, My Reflection', the modulations driven by the throb of the drum machine. The downfall of empires or a battle cry: whatever the music evoked, it felt empowering, and the dance floor grew ever busier, its figures enveloped in the thick emissions of the smoke machine. Its plumes were redolent of a metallic vanilla; unlike the heavily contaminated air of our city, one had the urge to inhale deeply before they dissolved.

Looking back, nearly everything about the scene felt ephemeral. A Baroque ephemeral. The Swiss art historian Heinrich Wölfflin once described the baroque as an expression above all of the 'tension of transience' – one shouldn't expect perfection or fulfilment from the baroque, he claimed, nor the static calm of being. Only the unrest of change. Wölfflin was attempting to describe the baroque line in art – restless and liberated and succumbing to an upward urge – yet I've often found that his words encompass many facets of Mexican culture. And not only Mexican culture, but adolescence itself, driven as it is by a sense of the fugitive, and a spilling over of emotions that constantly threaten to destabilise the present.

Adolescence is an encounter, indeed an ongoing

negotiation, with a self in transformation. Yet there's something undeniably alluring about unrest and, equally, about anything mutable and ephemeral and hard to pin down. Any fine experience is that more thrilling in the knowledge that at any moment it may well slip through our fingers, send us back to the mundane. Permanence doesn't inspire the same intoxication as does the fugitive, and somehow the atmosphere within El Nueve brought the tension of transience into relief. For the gay community it provided an inspiring space in which to enact extravagant dreams and simply feel free – not to mention that a few years earlier AIDS had arrived, exposing a deep-rooted homophobia within Mexican society – and for us teens, it was the site where our urges for nihilism and abandon could be lent a certain theatre.

In Mexico, as we have seen, three hundred years of colonial rule produced an art that was exuberant and excessive, in which emotionality seemed to triumph, every time, over restraint. El Nueve's aesthetic was similarly fed by a syncretism of European and Mexican cultures (and subcultures) – though of course without the tense backdrop of conquest and subjugation. In my memory I have always thought of it as a gay goth club. Was it truly goth? Perhaps not, apart from our *noches bugas*, which certainly were a *danse macabre* of skull rings and funereal garb. But my memory prefers to envision a space haunted by a spirit of mystery and concealment, emotions worn freely under a collective pall, silver crosses against a sky of black. Goth culture itself owes more than a little to the baroque – a love of contrasts and extremes, of monsters and hybrids, a celebration of the strange and marvellous, even an element of the carnivalesque. And, of course, the sense that any pleasure in life is stalked by the shadow of death.

Wearing black required little explanation: it stood for an internal weather, predominantly overcast, a heavy tilt towards melancholy that channelled a nineteenth-century Romanticism. Moonlight landscapes by Caspar David Friedrich, cues from Victorian mourning dress. Much of my own penumbral wardrobe came from Garage Union, a vast shop set up in a car park in West Berlin that sold clothes by the kilo. During the two summers our family spent in the city my sister and I would drop by weekly to scour the racks. Yet most of the clothes were dyed, and each time we washed them the water would run black, the garments slowly rinsed of their duskier shades. Much more permanent were the tattoos we got a few years later. We'd presented a copy of Edgar Allan Poe stories illustrated by the little-known German artist Wilfried Sätty, who often made montages inspired by the occult, and asked the tattooist to take the face of Roderick Usher and attach wings. The result was an androgynous angel, a curious marriage of goth and baroque, which has outlasted all the black.

That April night I remember looking around at the various characters on the dance floor, imagining how they would carry on with the same theatre long after I'd left to study abroad, and how these nights out, so charged with sorcery, would soon end. I had just kissed the Scottish DJ, a fully fledged goth from overseas, when our friend Jair cut his hand on a white metal trash can on the side of the dance floor. At first no one paid much attention – until it started gushing blood. Seeing that the matter required more light than what was on offer, a couple of us repaired to the Denny's diner on the corner. As we sat in a booth pressing napkins to Jair's hand, an elderly transvestite with painted eyebrows approached and, after seeing what was wrong, suggested rubbing cigarette ash in his wound. The man was charming and convincing, why not try, but Jair winced as soon as the ash came into contact with his wound. We hurriedly rinsed his hand in the bathroom and bandaged it up as best we could and, impatient to resume the night, returned to El Nueve.

A scuffle had erupted while we'd been gone. Two men were pushing each other threateningly, other men soon joined in and before long the scuffle exploded into a fury that threatened to swallow us all. Someone pulled out a gun. A bartender yelled out. Now, in the face of real death, all the young vampires went scurrying to find cover. Yoshua grabbed our hands and we flew down the stairs, past the bouncer at the entrance tensing up in anticipation of a fight, and into the parking lot across the street. We were about to climb into Yoshua's white car when one of the men came rolling down the ramp and before we knew it the brawl continued there. My sister and I quickly hid under the car, heads spinning, nausea on the rise. Bullets began crossing overhead. With our faces pressed against the damp cement, we breathed in the petrol and tried to block out the shouts and gunfire. When the fight moved into a corner of the parking lot we made a dash for it, jumped into the car and sped off.

We were already in our neighbourhood and had just turned off Reforma when, overcome by vertigo, I asked Yoshua to stop the car and let me out. I stumbled over to a tree and was breathing in some night air when all of a sudden two men came running out of the building in front of us, which we now realised was a bank, a bank that was being robbed. An alarm started sounding. My sister and

Yoshua yelled for me to get back into the car and off we sped a second time, as the moon, gazing down, shook her head.

Nights like these seem tame compared to now. Those had been small-scale criminals, most likely, or local drug dealers, and in the late eighties the main blight on our nights out were Los Anti-Cristos, a gang with inverted crucifixes tattooed on their temples. Their leader would carry a sword sheathed in his cane and his sidekicks had chain belts they could remove in combat; they listened to the same music we did and often turned up at our haunts to pick fights on the dance floor. Yet overall there reigned a sense of solidarity, particularly since the disastrous earthquake of 1985 and our then president's gross mishandling of the catastrophe. This led to a massive social mobilisation, and civilians of all ages had quickly teamed up to assist in the search for survivors.

That autumn Rockotitlán, the first large venue for live music, had opened, followed by places like Tutti Frutti and the LUCC. The alternative Mexican bands at the time – Caifanes, La Maldita Vecindad, Santa Sabina, Café Tacuba – reflected the ideals of young civil society and the social movements to come, and most musicians became fervent supporters of the Zapatistas.

I once described the music of my youth as a twilight always waiting to unfurl, but now that darkness has dramatically deepened in tone. In the years after I left Mexico, drug cartel violence spun out of control and journalists began being gunned down on streets across the country. The turbulent 1990s saw the Zapatista uprising, NAFTA (Mexico thrown open to global trade and influence), the weakening of the PRI, economic collapse and a series of high-profile political assassinations. Gruesome stories and their images have been a daily presence in the papers ever since.

The spectacle of El Nueve was indeed like a *danse macabre*, but while the *danse macabre* of medieval Europe was a cultural assimilation of the horrors of the Black Death, in our culture it prefigured the horror rather than assimilated it. In the late eighties, macabre iconography resided above all in our mood and our music and, more ancestrally, in the stone gods in the Museum of Anthropology.

How unusual that April night had been, yet how normal it had seemed at the time: a gunfight, an ageing transvestite professing shamanic powers, a bank being robbed before our eyes: everything veering into the carnivalesque, the Dionysian tinged by barbarity and hyperbolised emotion . . . When I returned home I knocked on my parents' door to let them know we were back and then lay down and tried to sleep, aware that soon these outings would come to an end. What I didn't know at the time was how bleak things would become, and how the aesthetic of our cultural choices somehow foreshadowed the events to unfold – still unfolding – in our country. In Mexico skulls no longer conjure up goth-y anthems from the eighties or the metaphysics of pre-Hispanic times; they now appear in mass graves, or as decapitated heads tossed onto a dance floor.

(El Nueve closed a few months after I left Mexico, in December 1989. On a recent visit home, I returned to the site. The building is now boarded up; its last incarnation was a bar called Ghost.)

Portrait
Gallery

Into the Laboratory: Aby Warburg

Most photographs of Aby Warburg show a dark-eyed, melancholy man, his gaze distant and withdrawn; in others, he exudes a manic energy. The eldest son of a Jewish banking dynasty from Hamburg, Warburg was born in 1866. His four brothers went into the family firm, but he was more interested in other sorts of currency and traded in his birthright for a limitless supply of books. Absorbed in academic pursuits yet working outside any institution, he regarded himself as an independent scholar rather than a professorial historian. Today he is perhaps less known for his writings (his subject was the early Renaissance) and more for the creation of an extraordinary library, now housed in the Warburg Institute in London, and the *Bilderatlas Mnemosyne*, both models of his mind in all its febrile cross-pollination.

The *Bilderatlas* (picture atlas) was an ever-evolving display of almost a thousand photographic images, mostly black and white, ranging from Babylon to Weimar Germany – with long stopovers in ancient Greece and the Renaissance – spread out over sixty-three numbered panels covered in black hessian cloth. Warburg juxtaposed reproductions of artworks with astronomical and astrological charts, maps, diagrams, advertising brochures, newspaper clippings, postage stamps and photographs, in an attempt to create something like a flow chart of Western civilisation, mapping the migratory routes of images with their writhing undertow of human drama and emotion.

It is strange to encounter Warburg in the sleek, chilly exhibition hall of the Haus der Kulturen der Welt (HKW), the oyster-shaped arts centre in Berlin where they chose to reconstruct the atlas from its last, and quite advanced, version of 1929. The lighting is dim and the panels are suspended from thin metal wires, casting rhomboid shadows on the floor – a control and geometry far from the time travel of the London Institute, with its exuberant shelves (books catalogued by theme across four floors: Image, Word, Orientation, Action), footed filing cabinets and centrifugal spirit. In order to recreate the *Bilderatlas* the curators, Axel Heil and Roberto Ohrt, sifted through 400,000 images, organised by motif, cross-referencing the vast Warburg archive against images and accounts of the 1929 atlas. After three months they had managed to locate around eighty per cent of the original photographs (the other images were reproduced) and found ways of remaining faithful to his affinities: the arrangement of panels is elliptical – the reading room of Warburg's Hamburg library was modelled after Kepler's ellipse, the transition from an astrological to an astronomical view of the cosmos – and sinuous: Warburg became interested in the serpent motif from early on, tracing its undulations through the waves of mythological seascapes, drapery, veils and coiled hair.

In the four years before his death in 1929, Warburg

would shuffle these images back and forth across the boards, using them for lectures and for research, a sort of workshop or laboratory in which he was able to illustrate different progressions of thought. His eccentric methods are well documented by his assistant Fritz Saxl, who described the way Warburg's research was animated by the tactile handling of documents and their visual display; constantly rearranged his books, too, mapping possible paths of conjecture. Each new idea called for a regrouping of the relevant volumes. He kept his personal notes in card boxes, the *Zettelkästen*, and constantly reshuffled these as well, spreading them across a table. Exceptional importance was attached to the placement of objects on his desk, as if it were a map of the cosmos.

At the HKW show, Warburg's archive is unpacked, his library distilled, his tools laid out before us. There is madness in the method but also evidence of a brilliant, obsessive mind who departed from the nineteenth-century approach to art history in favour of a non-linear, interdisciplinary reading that drew heavily on psychology and ethnography, his theories advanced through the spatial arrangement of images. Booklets providing captions to the images are available at the entrance to the exhibition but apart from these, and a few introductory texts, there is little explication. The effect is dreamlike, ghostly and elusive. From a distance some panels resemble a deconstructed frieze, or funerary stele. As you draw closer, you become aware of the many strange marriages and collisions. Warburg believed that modernity was haunted by an irrational, pagan antiquity, a kind of mythopoeic thought that held everything together.

The opening three panels, A to C, are the nerve centre

of the *Bilderatlas*, from which all the following panels unfurl. Panel A shows a map of astrological figures, a diagram
of cultural exchange routes in Europe and a genealogical
tree of the Tornabuoni, a Renaissance banking family –
'different systems of relationships, cosmic, earthly, genealogical, in which humanity is involved'. Panel B features
images from the zodiac, Hildegard von Bingen's *Scivias*,
Leonardo's *Vitruvian Man* and magical compendia –
'different degrees in the application of the cosmic system
to mankind'. Panel C displays Kepler's planetary orbits
and a medieval vision of Mars juxtaposed with newspaper
clippings of the *Graf Zeppelin* that crossed the Atlantic in
1929: early fantasies of outer space border a new techno-
logical age in the conquest of the sky.

Nearly all the panels feature human figures, or gods that
resemble humans, or human-animal hybrids. The mood
swings between ecstasy and melancholy, undercut by cur-
rents of violence. Panel 41a features more than a dozen
representations of Laocoön, the Trojan priest who was
strangled to death, along with his sons, by two immense
sea serpents – a punishment from Athena for warning the
Trojans about the wooden horse. The Laocoön sculpture
excavated in Rome in 1509 isn't depicted, but rather its
uncanny precursors and later iterations: Warburg wanted
to show that 'if the Laocoön hadn't been excavated, [the
people of the Renaissance] would have had to invent it'.
One engraving shows Laocoön standing with arms raised
as he fights off the snakes; in others he's seated, contorted
in pain. His expression ranges from fury to despair to restraint or resignation. Warburg was greatly influenced by
Gotthold Lessing's essay on Laocoön, the central text of
the German Enlightenment, and particularly by the idea

that an emotion such as agony could be represented in a whole range of modes. He gave the name Pathosformeln to the recurring gestures, or symptoms, that carve a path of social memory across different forms of representation: a certain pose, say, migrating from a tomb carving to a postage stamp. Images were, he thought, uniquely expressive of emotional undercurrents often lost to textual history.

The smaller displays behind the snaking panels offer glimpses into the physical world surrounding the *Bilderatlas*: photographs of the atmospheric Kulturwissenschaftliche Bibliothek in Hamburg, where, despite Warburg's mistrust of technology ('having enslaved electricity, captured lightning in the copper wire, man has created a culture that leaves no room for poetry'), the building was fitted in his absence with over twenty phones, a conveyor belt for books and a pneumatic post system. In 1921 it was converted into a research institute. A display of the versos of certain images (the life less glimpsed), many with Warburg's own handwritten annotations, key words and inscriptions, allows us to trace the journey of an image through the archive, identifying the places it previously occupied, the ideas it illustrated. Along the facing wall hangs a copy of an earlier version of the atlas: twice removed from the source, it has an even more spectral presence than the 'final' iteration.

A parallel and much smaller exhibition at the Gemäldegalerie has assembled fifty of the original works reproduced in the *Bilderatlas*, all from Berlin museums, allowing us to visualise certain aspects of Warburg's method and scholarship. The hierarchy of artworks is reinstated, emphasising the way he distorted images to suit his purposes, scaling up and scaling down, zooming in and out, cropping, editing, manipulating. At the Gemäldegalerie, a coin no longer has the same dimensions as a sculpture; here, you can discern the horses in Rembrandt's *Abduction of Proserpina*.

Warburg was obsessed with the figure of the nymph and created a weird sisterhood of menacing and alluring maidens, all portrayed with dynamic folds in their garments. The curators chose to exhibit a sinister bronze statue of a three-faced Hecate without the pedestal under her raised foot in order to highlight her instability, a precarious stance echoed by Ghirlandaio's Judith and Filippino Lippi's Erato nearby. One early eighteenth-century Norwegian bridal box, with primitively drawn interlocking figures, had lain in storage for many years, displayed only once, in the 1990s. At the HKW I'd hardly noticed it, eclipsed by other images on Panel 32: jaunty Morris dancers and Dürer's engraving of dancing monkeys. The real box depicts a curious scene, the Battle for the Trousers, in which seven women fight over a pair of trousers. Warburg related the image back to a passage in Isaiah, in which the shortage of men in Zion causes a fight to break out among a group of women. He bought the box on one of his collecting trips and later donated it to the Museum Europäischer Kulturen. Something mysterious rattles about inside; once the show is over, the curators are planning to pry open the lid.

Warburg described Burckhardt and Nietzsche, two of the figures who most influenced his thought, as 'highly sensitive seismographs' whose inner convulsions mirrored those of their times. As he attempted to reveal the unconscious life of images, his own nervous symptoms became more pronounced. In 1918, exhausted by war and what he saw as the collapse of civilisation, he suffered a breakdown and spent almost six years in institutions, most significantly at the Bellevue sanatorium in Kreuzlingen, a clinic run by the Swiss psychiatrist Ludwig Binswanger, the founder of 'existential analysis' ('the *Dasein* is not the individual; it is the background upon which the individual emerges').

Far from his library, Warburg worked in notebooks, filling dozens with often indecipherable pencil scrawls – threads unravelling and cascading down the page. Psychotic episodes alternated with lucid spells. The philosopher Ernst Cassirer visited him at the clinic; they discussed his library, of which Cassirer had become a willing 'prisoner', as well as Kepler and the ellipse. Other interlocutors included the moths that flew into Warburg's room at night. In letters he described them as his *Seelentierchen*, his little soul animals. Georges Didi-Huberman writes of the way in which the insects, with their erratic, exploratory flight paths, anticipated the *Bilderatlas* in its exploration of the dynamic tension of images set against a nocturnal backdrop. And it was at Kreuzlingen that Warburg delivered his Serpent Ritual lecture, inspired by a visit to the Hopi Indians in New Mexico and Arizona nearly thirty years earlier. Although absent from the *Bilderatlas*, it was an experience that reinforced his belief that the magical thinking of 'primitive' man was still present, sublimated into art and ritual. Here the snakes from Laocoön came alive, writhing in the hands of dancers and echoed in representations of lightning bolts.

As he recovered, Warburg began to confront the grief and calamity so deeply rooted in the culture he'd devoted his lifetime to studying. His reading became increasingly steeped in anthropology and psychology, his focus centred on humanity's primal, irrational urges. The *Bilderatlas* is the landscape of these final years, a battleground of reason and unreason. He referred to the project as an 'iconology of the interval', and it is the empty spaces in the panels, filled with unknown and uncertain matter, that hold the images in constellations of thought.

In the last three panels, the present day begins to intrude. An advertisement for body lotion in Panel 77 shows an airborne girl carrying a laurel wreath beside the words *Sieg der Jugend* (Victory of Youth). Somewhere around her floats Delacroix's *Medea* and scenes from *The Massacre at Chios*, as well as timetables for a North Sea ferry and postage stamps of Queen Victoria in the shell carriage and King George V as Neptune. Panel 78 charts the rise of Mussolini; Warburg was in Rome in 1929 and witnessed what he called its 'repaganisation'. The final panel includes a photograph of a hara-kiri ceremony, two late fifteenth-century depictions of the desecrations of the host by Jews, photographs of Catholic masses celebrating Mussolini and front pages of newspapers depicting images of golfers and, again, Il Duce. The *Bilderatlas* was forged under the sign of Mnemosyne but also pre-empted the violence of the Shoah and other tragedies of the twentieth century.

Warburg died of a heart attack on 26 October 1929, aged sixty-three. In an increasingly hostile climate – the Bauhaus evacuated, bonfires of books in Berlin, letters delivered to the Warburg library calling it a 'nest of Jews' – his family and librarians had to quickly decide on the fate of the collection. An English connection, and the insistence of Saxl, meant London was chosen as the place of exile.

In December 1933, sixty thousand books and fifteen thousand photographs were shipped over on the *Hermia*. The library furnishings followed in January.

At the far end of the HKW exhibition hangs a row of portraits of the various directors of the Warburg Institute, custodians of the collection and his legacy. Most fiercely loyal of all was Gertrud Bing, who had accompanied Warburg on his travels to Italy and who, along with Saxl, made many of the major posthumous decisions concerning the archive. She carried on Warburg's taxonomical work, grouping the images into categories and subcategories. Yet his reputation was contested among his heirs. When Ernst Gombrich called him a 'man lost in a maze', Edgar Wind rose to his defence: 'No doubt there was some obsessional quirk in Warburg's over-extravagant habit of preserving all of his superseded drafts and notes, thus swelling his personal files to gargantuan proportions, with comic side effects that did not escape him.'

Warburg intended the *Bilderatlas* to be published in three volumes – one volume of images and two of historical and critical commentary – and modelled it after the illustrated atlases of the late nineteenth and early twentieth centuries. Like Walter Benjamin's *Arcades Project*, to which it is frequently compared, it could never truly be completed. But its fragmentary and elliptical character doesn't diminish it – quite the opposite. It is all the more fascinating for being inherently melancholic, incantatory and unresolved (Matthew Vollgraff of the Warburg Institute calls it a modernist ruin); by reconstructing the atlas, the curators have revived it as a site of contemplation. Of the abundant supplementary text Warburg was intending, only a few cryptic notes exist, leaving it open to endless interpretation. Warburg himself remains an elusive figure onto whom it is easy to project one's own theories and obsessions. We can approach his final vision, the *Bilderatlas*, as an archaeological artefact or as an instrument of inquiry.

I Am Many:
Beatrice Hastings

Within Modigliani's oeuvre there are few objects and even fewer landscapes. Occasionally, a door or an item of furniture establishes an interior but most of the time the only narrative is the inner drama supplied by a face, the position of the hands, the tilt of a head. Early paintings depicted caryatids but soon these were freed from their architecture and given something more abstract to support. Charged with a dormant theatricality, his figures often resemble marionettes at rest. Modigliani intended to be a sculptor; inspired and encouraged by Brancusi, he started carving heads from stone. Before long, however, health and money troubles led him to abandon sculpture: fits of coughing due to childhood tuberculosis sabotaged the steady hand while dust from the stone irritated his lungs; during the war, marble became scarce and stone rose in price. He changed medium but not style, and replicated, in paint, the angularity of his three-dimensional figures.

Among the portraits Modigliani painted in his short lifetime, perhaps the least puppet-like were those of Beatrice Hastings, his partner from 1914 to 1916. In the two years of their stormy, brawl-filled romance, he painted her fourteen times. Yet for Modigliani, the two years with Hastings marked a surge in focus and creativity, and co-incided with his return to painting. For Hastings too, the time with him marked the most sustained and productive period of her work.

From their very first encounter, Modigliani was drawn to the English writer, referred to in Paris as 'la poétesse an-glaise'. As a devoted reader of Dante, he was also seduced by Beatrice's name. Poets already featured in his life and he'd painted them all: three years earlier he'd had a ro-mance with the melancholy Anna Akhmatova; his drink-ing companion was Blaise Cendrars; he knew Max Jacob and Jean Cocteau. By most accounts, he was never without a book in his pocket, usually Lautréamont's *Les Chants de Maldoror*.

Even within the bohemian milieu of Paris in the 1910s, Hastings and Modigliani made a feral, wayward pair. He lived in a haze of intoxication – absinthe, wine, hashish – and would dance on tabletops, howl out lines of Italian verse, riot through the streets at night. Hastings, mean-while, extravagant in dress and often accessorised with a basket of live ducks as a handbag, had forged a reputation as one of the main voices of *The New Age*, a British socialist journal of art and politics whose publisher A.R. Orage had been her partner for seven years. Her affairs with Kath-erine Mansfield and Wyndham Lewis had contributed to their eventual split, and in 1914 she moved to Paris as its correspondent, embarking on a series of chronicles enti-tled 'Impressions of Paris'. Through Max Jacob she rapidly gained entry into artistic circles, and before long formed part of what Malcolm Bradbury would call 'the standing

British atelier population in Paris who became points of contact and transmission'.

By then Hastings had already published under a wide spectrum of pen names. Beatrice Tina was the poet who often drew on mythological themes (most famously in the poem 'The Lost Bacchante'), and an outspoken champion of the Suffrage movement. In bold contrast was the essayist D. Triformis, a detractor of the Suffragettes and of Beatrice Tina herself. T.K.L., meanwhile, was a critic who parodied art movements, and quarrelled publicly with Ezra Pound while penning a parody of Marinetti's Futurist manifesto. Alice Morning was the Paris diarist (and her most developed and consistent voice). At other moments she was Pagan, Cynicus, Robert à Field, Mrs. Malaprop or G. Whiz. When one became troublesome, she would shed that persona and craft a new one. Encompassing them all was 'Beatrice Hastings' – itself the pseudonym of Emily Alice Beatrice Haigh, born in England in 1879 and raised in South Africa, who, after falling out with her family and a brief marriage to a boxer, returned to Europe in time for Modernism's heyday.

She had as many faces as voices. Modigliani's portraits together convey a shape-shifting, highly volatile nature: here, she stands in the threshold of a doorway, birdlike, with an inordinately long neck and a plume tucked behind her ear; there, she sits in the mesh of a gilt armchair, shadows rising off her like a headdress; hatted or unhatted, glimpsed frontal, profile or three quarters; in dark reds, oranges and umber. Her face is sometimes lean, more often round and strong-chinned. In one portrait, she's clad in a checked pale blue shirt with white collar, her pointy doll face and fluted lips strikingly similar to Modigliani's

Self-Portrait as Pierrot. Elsewhere, she is Madame Pompadour, the rim of her feathered black hat sailing across her forehead. In another portrait she looks precariously stitched up, as if with one tug of the thread her whole being might unravel, her absent eye like the missing button of a worn, over-loved toy.

Their domestic world was agitated yet creatively ablaze; the outside world was rocked by war. Often Hastings and Modigliani would wake to the thunder of bombs. During the winter siege, along with many other starving artists, they visited the soup kitchens. The tone of her dispatches from Paris darkened from light-hearted cultural chronicles to more serious reportage. After nearly two years, they parted ways, unable to accommodate their affairs and Beatrice's growing love of whiskey.

In early 1920 Modigliani's tuberculosis came roaring back and he died, destitute, aged thirty-five. Back in England, Hastings continued to write, albeit in more isolated conditions. The year Modigliani died, her own health worsened and she entered a clinic; a journal, later published as *Madame Six*, interweaves her Paris reminiscences, never far, with details of her hospital routine. Man Ray's photograph of her from 1922 depicts a gloomy character: jaw clenched, gaze sad and evasive, all self-possession and serenity gone from the face. Her interest in Theosophy deepened, particularly her devotion to Madame Blavatsky, whom she considered a kindred spirit, and in 1937 she published an impassioned defence.

'Civilised woman wants something more than to be the means to man's life: she wants to live herself.' Despite doing her best to honour this credo, Hastings ultimately faded into obscurity, ending her days in fevered, fragile solitude.

In 1943, she gassed herself in a small house in Worthing, a pet mouse cradled in her hand. Her death hardly earned a mention in the press, apart from the local paper.

Hastings's final Paris persona was Minnie Pinnikin, the eponymous narrator of an unfinished novella in which she detailed her relationship with Modigliani. Pinnikin: a portmanteau, possibly, of pinnacle and mannequin, capturing the moment in her life when Hastings found herself at the peak of her craft while existing as the central model in someone else's.

Varieties of Exile: Mavis Gallant

Food may have been an ongoing preoccupation during Mavis Gallant's first years of travelling around Europe living hand to mouth, but once her writing career was launched in the 1950s and food readily available, meals became more about conversation than nourishment. You could argue that Mavis was, above all, nourished by social interaction and an almost anthropological study of others – an opportunity that lent itself nicely around the dinner table. I recall one meal in particular, at my parents' home in Paris in 2010, while my father was Mexican ambassador to UNESCO. A series of photographs taken that day depict her face mirrored in a silver charger, in an image that also captures the fleeting, illusory nature of permanence in a diplomatic residence.

Mavis reflected in a disc of borrowed silver: the face looking into the camera is vivid and complete; the face in the plate is distorted and at one degree of remove. One acknowledges us, the other peers into mysterious depths we cannot see. I cannot help but envision this double portrait, at times, as emblematic of her life as an émigré. After leaving her native Canada in her early twenties, Mavis spent more than six decades in Paris. Yet her work never stopped addressing themes of displacement. She had a splendid voice that defied the passage of time – girlish and from another era – and she often addressed people as 'dear'. That day, we ate and she spoke, humoured by her anecdotes from a distant past, occasionally poking at the cheese soufflé in her plate as it succumbed to gravity. Her manners were delicate and birdlike, and the touch of her hands, I recall, was wonderfully soft.

The previous autumn, we'd taken her to the Louvre to see the exhibition 'Titian, Tintoretto, Veronese: Rivals in Renaissance Venice' (Venice itself, of course, a city of reflections, from the canals to the Renaissance armour). Mavis had been studying the paintings from the height of the wheelchair we'd procured for her at the entrance. She paused for a long time in front of Titian's *Venus with Mirror* (c. 1555), the mirror tall and flat, unlike the round convex ones widely used by the Flemish at that time.

In our portrait of Mavis, most of the cutlery has been removed and only the small fork and spoon remain, suggesting the main course has been eaten and we are waiting for dessert. I no longer recall what it was that evening, though it probably involved some variation of chocolate; Mavis was diabetic but she loved sweets.

A few years later, once my parents had returned to Mexico and I had moved to London, I visited Mavis in her flat in the sixth arrondissement. It was to be the last time I'd see her; she died in 2014. One of her first questions was, where was I staying? At a friend's house, I replied, which was a bit run-down and full of spiders. With the mention of spiders something was triggered, and they quickly became the *leitmotif* of the afternoon. Each time Mavis spoke, she would include them in the sentence, either in her replies or else to address an imaginary spider at the window. Her thoughts travelled back in time to her childhood in Canada, where she and her brother once found a large spider in their house, then returned to the present to the imaginary spider in her flat. Telling it to go outside, she was now very concerned with the seen and unseen in her home.

At one point she stood up and asked me to follow her to look at a favourite painting on the wall: a strange, dreamlike scene, in muted colours, featuring a seated man gazing down at a bundle, perhaps a dog, in his lap while a hatted young woman, in profile, stands to one side of him. Beside her, another woman, with large earrings and a long green skirt, reads out from a book as other figures hurry past. 'I always thought it was about a girl who had been waiting for someone who never showed up,' Mavis explained, then sat back down.

Revisiting these photographs of her face reflected in

the dinnerware, I feel again the magnitude of her gaze –
playful, kind, intelligent, slightly enigmatic. To her right
sits a full glass of water, glinting with light from the chan-
delier. Perhaps she has been sipping at it and it's been
recently refilled, or has it, in the midst of so much conversation and observation, been forgotten over the course of
the meal?

A Life Remembered: Chiki Weisz

At night in the dark he would see figures crossing his room speaking Hungarian.

He'd had a dog named Maroush whom he would walk daily.

He never learnt English, his wife's mother tongue; until the end, they spoke French.

He loved playing dominoes with his nurse or sons or any friend that came by.

Supper was instant oatmeal mixed with Coffeemate and hot water, to which he'd add canned peaches in syrup and two sliced miniature bananas, and a few strands of cheese he'd eat with toothpicks as if at a reception.

For fifty years he'd been the official photographer at the Rotary Club and lunched there on weekdays.

He was never without his black beret. The street children called him Manolete.

He would doze in a chair with a blanket up to his chin and a Siamese cat in his lap.

He'd arrived in Mexico by ship in 1941, one of many European émigrés to find sanctuary in its capital.

Most of his family had been murdered in the Holocaust.

He would watch wildlife programmes on television and when the antenna didn't work he would watch the snowy screen.

In 1938 he had walked from Budapest to Paris with Robert Capa, for whom he'd worked as darkroom manager. He saved thousands of Capa's negatives in three suitcases and brought them to Mexico. They were discovered only in 2008.

'He is still here,' his wife said after he passed away. No one ever sits in his chair at the kitchen table.

His name was Emerico Weisz. They called him Chiki.

He was married to Leonora Carrington.

A Leonora Carrington A-Z

Ambidextrous: Leonora could write and paint with both hands at once, backwards and forwards. 'Yes, I'm ambidextrous, like madmen,' she once said.

Bullfighting: 'Horrific. It's a disgusting, shameful demonstration of human stupidity and cruelty. Horrible. I was once put out at a bullfight. I got up and clapped when the bull jumped over the thing and chased all the attendants around, and I just clapped and clapped, and they put me out.'

Cats: The last cats Leonora owned were Ramona and Monsieur, two green-eyed Siamese who followed her around the house. She wanted a dog too but worried the cats would stop speaking to her.

Devils: 'I think there are very dangerous devils, and I think there are interesting devils, and I think there are very stupid devils. I think there are probably intelligent ones, and angels and anything that has been invented. Hundreds, thousands of them, all over the place . . . Well, I use the word *invented* when I mean *seen*. I don't know what invented means, really, do you?'

England: Leonora would express nostalgia for England but at the same time no desire to return. She missed the trees and the architecture rather than the people, since most of those she knew had passed away, and the eventful moments of her life had taken place abroad.

Filters: Until her final days, Leonora smoked. Her choice of cigarette varied but she always attached them to short plastic filters, which she would clean and reuse.

Grey: More than anything, Leonora wore grey. Baggy grey trousers, long grey sweaters, grey shawls, grey turtlenecks, grey lace-up shoes. Occasionally she'd bring in a bit of purple but my memory of her is distinctly in monochrome.

Haunting: Leonora would sometimes mention a middle-aged woman in pink who'd appear in different rooms. A few friends claimed to have seen the ghost too, standing behind her. She was never scared, however; in previous times, her home had been a printing house, 'which is not a very sinister thing'.

Imagination: 'Nothing is created by the imagination. Imagination is a very mysterious force which we know very little about. We don't know if it creates anything . . . I think that things occur, like for instance somebody one time must have invented a cup, because it was easier than putting your face into a river and lapping up the water.'

James, Edward: Englishman in Mexico, patron of the Surrealists; Leonora was fond of him, despite saying he lacked respect for his friends and would wash his hands with her shampoo.

Kabbalah: The writings Leonora would mention most often, important to her throughout her lifetime.

Lapland: Often when we'd ask Leonora what place she would most like to visit she would reply, Lapland. She loved reindeer and wished the Laps would stop eating them.

Manipulation: She said manipulation is what makes 'the great cosmic yoghurt'.

Nagas: Some of Leonora's favourite mythical creatures, from Indian mythology, which featured in her paintings and sculptures.

Orange Pekoe: Leonora would often ask me to bring her a tin of tea from England, especially Orange Pekoe. She also loved PG Tips, 'bog standard English tea', and said she much preferred it to fancy teas. Whatever I brought her she would keep under lock and key so that no one else could use it. 'Cacher la boîte de PG Tips'.

Painting: 'I rarely paint images from dreams. Images occur just like that. They occur from something that is further away from my consciousness, I think. But any painter would tell you that.'

'Quel désir d'extravagance!': André Breton's words upon first seeing her paintings, in Paris when Leonora was twenty.

Roma: Colonia Roma was the neighbourhood where she lived from the 1940s; over the decades, it underwent an enormous transformation. Across the street lay the debris of a collapsed building, a victim of the 1985 earthquake, which housed a growing community of cats and homeless people. Leonora called it 'a garden of scorpions'.

Spiritism: Leonora could see through the hocus pocus of people who claimed to have supernatural powers. She once played a trick on a 'very serious ex-Nazi with a thick German accent' who held a séance – she brought along one of her sons and before the session they attached a small instrument to the bottom of the table. It made metallic noises whenever it was pulled by a string. Everyone sat down. After a while, Leonora began to grow bored and decided to play a trick on the ex-Nazi. She or her son pulled the string. Noises were heard coming from beneath the table. Leonora remarked, 'I think there's something there.' So the ex-Nazi asked, 'Who are you?' and she replied, 'I think it's a horse.' The man stood up and tipped the table over to reveal the hidden instrument. He never spoke to Leonora again.

Time: 'I don't need to kill time. It's killing me.' (When asked whether she played chess – uninterested in board games, she'd rather draw.)

University of contraception: Leonora's idea; she would often complain there were too many people in the world and wished they would establish such a university.

Varo, Remedios: Feline-faced Spanish painter, one of

Leonora's closest female friends, with whom she shared a love of cats.

Weisz, Emerico, also known as Chiki: Hungarian photographer to whom Leonora was married for over fifty years, largely in silence.

Xanax (Tafil in Mexico): Leonora would take half a tablet every night for sleep and anxiety. 'The darkness' would set in by late afternoon, she said.

Yeti: Leonora's final pet, a small white, hyperactive Maltese, for whom she had tremendous affection.

Zoology: Leonora adored animals, mythical and real. 'I draw completely from my mind. Well, I don't know if it's my mind . . . But if I'm drawing an animal like a cat, I'd like to draw it from life.'

Tea and Creatures with Leonora Carrington: A Photo Essay

Over time, even the numbers 194 on her front door seemed to grow more creaturely, the first gatekeepers one encountered upon arrival, followed by Leonora Carrington herself, swathed in grey. Her home in Mexico City was a chessboard of Mexican sunlight and European shadow – much of the house was stone-chilly and austere, but then you'd step into a patch of sun or come face-to-face with one of her sculptures, an eruption of life emerging from the murk. After a brief greeting, she would lead you from the entrance to the kitchen. The kettle would already be on, an old metal thing rattling over the fire, while her two Siamese cats, Monsieur and Ramona, silently patrolled the premises.

I took some photographs of her one afternoon as we sat having tea, struck by the procession of instruments hanging behind where Leonora was seated. Their shadows – evoking claws, shovels, tridents, horned creatures – were imbued with a *Fantasia* sorcerer's potential, and I half expected them to come alive and start marching around. I'm

not certain Leonora herself was even aware of this opti-
cal effect, which so aptly mirrored the co-existence of the
fantastical and the quotidian in her own work, and I don't
remember ever seeing such shadows again.

Looming out of the corners of her living room, one
of the duskiest regions of the house, were Leonora's oven
sculptures: tall bronze witnesses to her daily life. Created

from smaller models and then packed off to the foundry – in her words, 'a great alchemical laboratory' – they would return lengthened and transformed. Towering over everyone, the mask-like faces would stare out, radiating an enigmatic serenity, while down at each base a little door opened into a square compartment that could, ostensibly, be used as an oven, though I'm not sure anyone ever tried.

Leonora called this sculpture *ING* (*c.* 1994), as in cooking, paint-ing, see-ing: a sort of Golem figure, it represented the verb incarnate. In her world, everything might possess a soul; even grammar becomes an entity. When posing for this photograph, Leonora stood up straight and rested a hand on *ING*'s arm, her hint of a smile, gracious

and reserved, mimicking the creature's own. The framed cloudy window behind them gives the impression they have stepped out of a painting, emptying the canvas of its figures.

The final addition to Leonora's menagerie was Yeti, a lively Maltese dog who accompanied her during the last three years of her life, after her cats and husband had passed away. The last photograph I have of her was taken by my father in March 2011, two months before she died. The dog exists in the present, its gaze fastened on the plate of biscuits on the table, while Leonora's focus is on something beyond. Clutching her cigarette, she is aware of the camera yet doesn't acknowledge its presence. Her

expression is intense, indomitable. Behind her crouches an old stove – *ING*'s clunkier, once more functional, cousin – and, most important, the door to the kitchen: one of many charged thresholds in her home.

Uprooted: Encounters Between Mexican Flora and Its Foreigners

1937–1940

From collective struggle to individual survival, Leon Trotsky fills his garden in Mexico with cacti.

Staff accompany him into the mountains on the hunt for certain specimens. They dig up the heavy cacti, wrap them in newspapers, gather up the surrounding soil in bags, replant them in the garden.

Trotsky was probably unaware of what he was doing: brutal extraction, disturbance of earth, destruction of an underground network.

Cacti/cactus. How counterintuitive, that plural 'i' and the singular 'us'. The Aztecs used cacti as fences: tall, barbed columns to encircle homes and villages. In modern times too, cacti draw boundaries, demarcate spaces.

Trotsky's cacti weren't for protection. For that he had bars and steel shutters placed on the windows of his house and, after the first assassination attempt, added watchtowers to the garden wall. The prickly plants were ornaments, not sentinels; in his fortified prison, they stood more for expanse than restriction. Yet they also represented – vertical, monolithic, autonomous – an anchoring of place, and endurance.

1938

André Breton travels to Mexico. He claims he has been sent on a cultural mission but the real reason, friends say, is to meet Trotsky, whom he greatly admires. (They meet, take walks around Lake Pátzcuaro, and draw up 'Manifesto for an Independent Revolutionary Art', which is co-signed by Diego Rivera for security reasons.)

'A Surrealist country *par excellence*', is what Breton calls Mexico. It is therefore surprising that upon his return to France one of three presiding memories is that of a peasant in rags and a wide-brimmed hat, standing beside a giant cactus clutching a rifle. There is nothing alien or enigmatic about this image, nothing remotely Surrealist: it is staged, clichéd, folkloric. Yet the peasant's image is what endures, for the man embodies Trotsky's revolutionary ideals and therefore the inspiring conversations Breton had while in Mexico.

There is a great deal written about what happens when we come into contact with a cactus's painful spines but much less about what happens to the cactus when it comes into contact with a human. Like all fellow plants, cacti respond to stimuli. They feel the wrench when pulled out of the earth. Cactus theft, usually carried out under cover of the night, has become a serious problem, and threatens to destroy desert equilibrium in the southern United States and Mexico.

From Trieste to Veracruz, Emperor Maximilian and Empress Carlota travel onwards to Mexico City. At the end of their first night, despite the great pomp and ceremony with which they are received, bedbugs in the mattress at the national palace force the Emperor to sleep on a billiards table and the Empress in an armchair. It is an occupied country at war, resentful of foreign intervention. The bedbugs are the first tiny voice of dissent.

Throughout his time in Mexico, Emperor Maximilian enthuses to his courtiers about the native flora. An inquisitive man, he disembarks from the royal carriage to explore the land by foot. He admires the maguey and boasts of having first-hand experience of specimens that most naturalists in Europe, with the exception of Humboldt, only fantasise about.

Yet he is unaware of toloache.

Toloache / *Datura innoxia* is a nightshade with white trumpeted flowers and a prickly fruit. First used as a local anaesthetic, the Aztecs fed it to victims of human sacrifice before tearing out their hearts. In modern times it is used as an aphrodisiac. In high doses the plant wreaks havoc on the mind: great excitation followed by depression followed by disorientation and visual hallucinations.

For Empress Carlota, it certainly did not awaken any desire. She had shown signs of mental instability since childhood but legend has it toloache was the final trigger, and that a healer had given it to her to drink at the marketplace. Others said it was being slipped into her morning coffee. In any case, Mexico, its land and its sorcery, began to inhabit her more deeply. Native flora was brought 'indoors', where it swiftly colonised the individual.

Emperor Maximilian and Carlota were themselves viewed as a colonising force when in reality they were victims of a tragic situation imposed by Napoleon III, intent on expanding his empire overseas. In 1867 Maximilian was executed on the orders of Benito Juárez. Carlota returned to the melancholic castle of Miramare and thence to Bouchout Castle in Belgium. The madness continued to inhabit her, her mind a card shuffle of landscapes past and present.

Toloache is still easily found at marketplaces in Mexico, mixed into powders and potions that promise to kindle strong desire in the Other. In the United States the elusive Datura innoxia *is now considered an invasive plant, little more than a weed, spread easily on the fur of animals that have entered into contact with its spiny capsules. Because of its high toxicity, some countries have prohibited its sale or cultivation.*

1936

Antonin Artaud sails to Mexico, via Antwerp and Havana. He wrestles with the demons of morphine addiction withdrawal and excommunication, courtesy of Breton, from the Surrealist group. He travels north to the Sierra Madre Occidental, home to the Tarahumaras.

Artaud is drawn to the Tarahumaras' hermaphroditic principles, and to the peyote plant's hermaphroditic roots: two halves clasping each other, an image of completeness and self-sufficiency. He has long been haunted by the thought that he does not possess his mind in its entirety. He recognises something transcendent in the androgyne.

In the Tarahumaras' sacred lands he observes and partakes of their peyote ritual. It is a new kind of theatre.

Abjection. Compression. Disassociation.

Collapse ensues between inner landscapes and outer, another spell cast between the alien and the endemic.

Artaud is hostage not to historical events but to a mind preyed upon by *idées fixes*. Later on, he would ask for his name to be removed from his text about his voyage to the land of the Tarahumaras and substituted by three stars: * * * like peyote buttons.

The peyote faces habitat destruction as well as overharvesting for ceremonial use. It grows slowly, flowers sporadically and thrives in scrubby areas. If the crown with its buds is cut off too near the base, a common occurrence, the plant does not regenerate.

*

For the rest of her days, Carlota lived in fear of being poisoned. Trotsky, during his shorter life, lived in similar fear, though his end was delivered by an ice axe with a wooden handle and a sharp metal head, of the kind used by mountaineers. Back in France, Artaud was certain he'd been hexed in Mexico and lingered under the spell. He also complained that he was being poisoned by his doctors at the psychiatric clinics where he spent the final decade of his life. By then, the saturated colours of the peyote trip had been replaced by a palette of monotony, magic ritual by medical monstrosity. The ghosts of exotic vegetation are indifferent to time, place and struggle.

Map of a Lost Soul

Shortly before five, the figure on the bench starts to stir. She sits up and tightens her headscarf, then drops a hand to check that her bags are still on the ground by her feet. A bus hurtles past on one side of the spacious traffic island on which the bench is located. This long strip – populated by trees, wrought-iron benches and old-fashioned lamp-posts – bisecting Avenida Alvaro Obregón in one long green and cement declaration, is her home.

Local businesses have yet to open and most of Co-lonia Roma remains in shadow. The figure, severely hunchbacked, slowly moves from the bench to the twenty-four-hour shop across the street for her dawn cup of instant coffee. She rarely says a word but the employees know who she is: Margaret Aberlin, a sixty-five-year-old German woman who has been living on the streets of Mexico City for the past four years. Occasionally, when the tempera-ture drops, she arrives earlier and falls asleep standing by the coffee machines, leaning against the metallic counter until her legs give way.

She lingers for an hour until other customers start to arrive, then leaves in as much silence as she entered. Her next destination, six streets away, is the Sagrada Familia, a church on the corner of Puebla and Orizaba.

A soft dawn light is starting to touch the tips of trees and buildings as she continues on her route, which over four years has never varied: off Alvaro Obregón she turns into Orizaba, past dormant cars and shuttered entrances, then makes her way across the Plaza Río de Janeiro.

The plaza too has yet to awaken, its great trees stilled under the gaze of the giant statue of Michelangelo's *David*. Grand old houses, built in French style during the Porfiriato, hunch around the plaza, their occupants either asleep or inhabiting a dimension that doesn't know sleep. The air is chilly; Margaret Aberlin quickens her pace. She passes the bed of tall dark green cacti, which like sinister fingers rise from the soil and point up at the sky.

The street of Orizaba, which continues on the other side of the Plaza Río de Janeiro, brings her directly to the Sagrada Familia. This Romanesque Gothic church with its blue spire and large rosette window is the point of departure for the Procession of Silence, which takes place once a year on Good Friday, but for some it forms part of a daily procession.

It is now six, and its heavy wooden doors are being opened. Margaret steps into its luminous interior lit up by three fancy chandeliers – a hesitant light enters the stained-glass windows – and settles into the last pew near the confessional.

Her presence never fails to be registered by the caretaker, a frail man who sleeps in a tiny room at the back of the church behind the altar, no family or beloveds apart from the saints and evangelists adorning the walls. He often notices flowers sticking out of the woman's bag but assures himself they're different from the white ones in the vase arrangements.

Seated on the wooden pew, hard but certainly more comfortable than the cold metal of her park bench, Margaret sleeps until eleven, when the church closes until evening. Someone, either the caretaker or the sacristan, usually has to tap on her shoulder to wake her.

She shuffles out in her long brown leather jacket, pausing to receive some coins from the faithful, who are used to the sight of her. With some of these donations Margaret heads to the newspaper stand to one side of the church, its owner perched on an upturned crate, and buys two Tomy caramels and two Tehuanos, among the cheapest sweets at hand.

She has a very clean, sweet smell, the newspaper man always notes, unlike the vagrant woman who used to sit outside the Sagrada Familia. When this woman died, he said, the ambulance men had great difficulty lifting the stretcher, astonished at how much she weighed; they shook the folds of her filthy skirt, and out poured hundreds of coins.

From the church, Margaret Aberlin heads back down Orizaba. By now the streets have come to life and the sun has climbed the sky. At the hair salon at No. 27 a woman lays her scissors to one side and combs out the tangles of her next customer. At No. 29 two bodyguards spoon salsa onto their tacos while the man they protect lunches at a restaurant across the street. A young man fixes a bicycle outside No. 31. The shop two doors down is still closed since its owner has been feeling unwell.

Margaret stops at No. 35, a simple restaurant with a red awning she visits daily. She finds a seat in the corner and eats her usual ham and cheese sandwich, hunched over her food with her back to everyone.

Afterwards she moves on to La Bella Italia, an ice cream parlour back on Alvaro Obregón, furnished with retro tables and chairs and a jukebox that lights up whenever a song is played. The employees call her Margarita. Unless it is occupied, she always takes the same little round table by the window. Not once does she order ice cream, only an espresso, into which she empties two packets of sugar. She pulls a pack of cookies from her bag and eats them with the coffee, then spends over an hour flipping through magazines she's also pulled out of her bag. Sometimes she disappears into the bathroom and emerges in another set of clothes.

Over the years, they have come to know her story. At first they were surprised by her good Spanish, fluent with a German accent, and were told she also spoke French, English and of course German – a 'High German', which sounded impressive though they weren't certain what that meant.

Some days she wouldn't speak at all, on others she would ask the time, saying that any day now they'd be coming to fetch her. Who are coming, they'd ask? My husband and daughter, Margaret would reply; they will arrive on a private plane from Germany and from here we will fly to Buenos Aires and from there on to Hawaii. They had abandoned her while on holiday in Mexico, she said, but would be returning any day to fetch her.

When speaking, her blue eyes would light up and she'd smile. Yet on days when she didn't say a word her face remained unlit. The employees at La Bella Italia often tried to imagine what she'd looked like when she was young, but for some reason it was impossible.

From there Margaret Aberlin walks to her favourite place, a bookshop called A Través del Espejo – Through the Looking Glass. The owner knows her and expects her arrival at around the same time every afternoon. Stretching in long rows to the far end of the shop, high piles of books rise to the ceiling. The shelves lining the walls also brim with books. Wherever one turns, more and more books, following little apparent order or logic.

Here too, Margaret has her routine. She sits on a low stool and places her bags around her. First she leafs through a large stack of *National Geographic*, some issues from over a decade ago. Once she is done, she organises them in chronological order. Then she reaches for some books and once she is done looking at them she also organises them by publication date. Sometimes she points at the books and says to the owner, 'These are my books.' Sometimes she waves her hand and says, 'This is my bookshop.'

Whenever she comes across the issue of *National Geographic* with the iconic photograph of the Afghan girl on the cover, she holds it up and tells whoever is there that it is a portrait of her as a girl. Because of the similar light eyes, people often believe her. Every now and then she puts aside a novel or a collection of short stories written in one of the languages she knows. The owner usually lets her have the book for free, and in return, Margaret gives her a flower from her bag.

After the bookshop she drops by the local florist to replenish her collection. She doesn't purchase much but she knows what she wants. She prefers simple, rather than sunflowers or birds of paradise. Once she's paid, she drops the flowers into one of her plastic bags and continues on her way back to the traffic island on Alvaro Obregón, which is now much busier and noisier than in the morning when she left it.

The grand avenues have corners built at forty-five degrees, wide enough for carriages to once comfortably turn, and are visited at intervals by fountains with sculptures from Greek and Roman mythology. Always looking down, Margaret Aberlin seems blind to the neighbourhood's decaying elegance, the result of big earthquakes and bad decisions.

If ever there happens to be someone seated on her bench when she returns, she asks the person or persons to leave. She sits and closes her eyes. The minutes pass. Often her rest is punctuated by the sirens of ambulances pulling up to the Hospital Obregón across the street, fronted by the strange statue of a famous Mexican comic holding out his hand. Fortunately, despite medical attention being literally at her doorstep, she has never needed to go there.

In the late afternoon she heads to another restaurant for her main meal of the day, chicken broth with rice and a bottle of dark Bohemia beer.

Afterwards she returns to her bench, gathering leaves and bits of garbage along the way. She stuffs them into her bags, where she also carries old newspapers, clothing and a pair of shoes.

From the second-floor window of a building on Alvaro Obregón, an ageing jeweller, who lives there with her unemployed son, has been watching Margaret Aberlin for the past four years. During the day, a gold lamé dress hangs in the window. At night, the dress is brought indoors and the window is closed, shutting out noise, shutting in fantasies.

The ageing jeweller is deeply intrigued by this humped woman, who she sees rising in the morning, returning to her bench at intervals during the day and then lying down at night. She herself is wasting away from an unidentified disease and hasn't left her home in nine months. Her son brings her food and things to read, carefully wheels her from room to room, but has no idea that his mother follows the comings and goings of someone beyond the window.

In the early evening, Margaret Aberlin returns to the Sagrada Familia.

Every now and then as she crosses the Plaza Río de Janeiro she walks past a retired organ grinder, member of a dying breed. For five decades he played outside Bellas Artes, cranking out traditional songs like 'Cielito Lindo' and 'Las Mañanitas', but over the years the imported brass cylinders have become harder to replace and fewer people stopped to listen to his song. Like most barrel organs in Mexico, his was made in the early twentieth century by an Italian named Frati, based in Berlin.

The organ grinder sits by the statue of David polishing his instrument when a hunched woman in a long leather jacket stops and stares. At first he thinks she is admiring the shiny black of the oak but he then realises she is staring in wonderment at the gold lettering on the side:

HARMONIPAN
FRATI & CO. SCHOENHAUSER ALLEE 73 BERLIN

She stands and stares, silently clutching her bags, and eventually continues on her way.

Shortly after they reopen the Sagrada Familia, Margaret Aberlin is back, ready to resume her place on the pew in the final row near the confessional. She listens to the organ music, which soothes her, but has told people that all the talk of death during mass makes her sad.

She remains in the church until it closes at nine.

Back down Orizaba, through the darkened Plaza Río de Janeiro, where shadows congregate round the fountain, she heads towards a mini supermarket for her supper: instant Maruchan chicken soup – to which she adds coffee instead of boiling water. For all her meals she uses the same plastic spoon, which she pulls out of a bag and disinfects with alcohol and a napkin. After eating she stores it away again.

By eleven Margaret Aberlin is back at her bench, ready for bed. Sometimes when she returns she encounters someone sitting there, whom she must shoo away. She waves her hand and tells them she needs to go to sleep. She tucks her bags under the bench and then lies down, resting her head on a folded sweater. Her thick leather jacket protects her against the cold of the metal. Cars continue to hurtle past on either side of her island, but with the hours the traffic diminishes. And there she remains, most nights, until five, when her daily routine begins again.

Along with the ageing jeweller, she is often observed by a street kid who has taken up residence somewhere beneath the massive underpass of the Insurgentes roundabout. On some nights, however, when it gets too noisy, he too goes to sleep on a bench on the Alvaro Obregón traffic island, and it is then that he has witnessed the foreign woman bathing in one of the fountains. It is a strange sight, a deformed figure cupping water over her head alongside the poised classical statues, and he watches in fascination, hoping they'll somehow converge, like the satyr and the nymph.

One morning when the jeweller looks out her window she notices a commotion engulfing the bench. A crowd has gathered. Through her open window she hears voices above the traffic. Two men are trying to lift the woman from the bench. She resists, clasping the side with both arms. But they are stronger and eventually wrench her away and push her into a car. At first her bags get caught in the door and they have to manoeuvre them in at an angle. The door closes and the car drives off. All that remains are two bent flowers beneath the bench.

The jeweller's son, who is more informed than she realises, tells her that night over dinner that this woman, whose presence he too was aware of though not following as closely, has been taken away to be 'repatriated'. All because earlier that month a leading newspaper had published an article about a German woman who lived on a bench in Colonia Roma – 'She sleeps standing and adds coffee to her soup', was the headline – and thanks to this, the German embassy had been alerted to her existence. After a few weeks of tireless research, someone there was able to track down her family in Germany. Most of her story, it turned out, was true: four years ago, Margaret Aberlin had been abandoned by her husband and daughter while on holiday in Tepoztlán.

After two weeks held at the migratory detention centre in Iztapalapa, where she refused all phone calls and visitors, Margaret Aberlin was released at seven in the evening and driven to the international airport of Mexico City, where she boarded Air France flight 439 to Paris. She refused to bring any of her bags along. Her brother would be waiting at the other end to take her to their hometown of Bad Oeynhausen.

Last Recital: Dinu Lipatti

Aware it would be his final performance, he chose his programme carefully: Bach's Partita No.1 in B-flat Major, Mozart's Sonata No. 8 in A Minor, Schubert's Impromptus in G-flat Major and E-flat Major, and Chopin's waltzes. All pieces he loved and, despite his legendary modesty, knew he had mastered. Radiodiffusion Française had planned to broadcast the recital live but pulled it at the last minute for fear he would fail. Thankfully, they had the presence of mind to record it.

It was early autumn, 16 September to be exact, 1950, and the third year of the Besançon music festival. Dinu Lipatti arrived by car, accompanied by his wife, Madeleine. He'd been particularly weak that month and running a fever. His doctors implored him to cancel yet he insisted on honouring the engagement.

His body was ravaged by a seven-year battle with Hodgkin's lymphoma. He had recorded less than four hours of music in his lifetime; perhaps he sensed this final offering would, in one way or another, seal his legacy. He was helped onto the stage and led to his piano. Photographs show not a single free seat in the hall.

He could not fail. He would not fail.

In the Bucharest villa where he'd grown up, music had been the only god. His father was a violinist, his mother a pianist, and their prayers for a musical son were answered early on. Whenever his mother felt the baby kicking inside her womb, she would say he was pressing down on the piano pedals. His baptism was held not at birth but at his second birth, when he learnt to play the instrument. At the ceremony, attended by his godfather George Enescu, he astonished everyone by playing a Mozart minuet. At three and a half, nothing could budge Constantin 'Dinu' Lipatti from the piano. By the age of four he'd begun developing back pains from so many hours at the keys.

Lipatti excelled at the conservatory in Bucharest, where he studied under the great pianist and pedagogue Florica Musicescu and won prizes. In 1934 he earned second place at an international piano competition in Vienna; Alfred Cortot resigned from the jury to protest he hadn't been given the top award. Lipatti moved to Paris to continue studying, now under the supervision of Cortot and Nadia Boulanger, as well as Paul Dukas and Charles Munch. He met his fellow Romanian pianist Clara Haskil, with whom he developed a close friendship.

He also composed his own music, a heady blend of French neoclassicism and Romanian folk; his symphonic suite *The Gypsies* was awarded a silver medal in France. During quieter moments he nurtured a passion for photography. Ever ready to indulge him, his mother set up a darkroom but worried the chemicals would harm his most treasured possession. Fully grown, his hands could comfortably span a twelfth.

At nineteen, he began recording. Unaware of how brief

his life would be, he was cautious and took his time, practicing each piece tirelessly before committing it to vinyl. It was unusual to find a musician whose personality did not intervene. His humility, the purity and reverential detachment of his playing, was commented on by everyone. For Yehudi Menuhin he was a 'manifestation of the spiritual realm'. Poulenc called him 'an artist of divine spirituality'. Herbert von Karajan: 'This wasn't about the piano. This was Music, all earthly weight cast off; Music in its purest form, with the harmony that can only be given by someone . . . who is already no longer quite with us.'

Yet the standards Lipatti set himself were so high he was never truly satisfied. His father bought him a Bechstein concert piano, which he would play at the family retreat in Fundateanca. That is where he was happiest, his mother would write, seated at his Bechstein, surrounded by nature, with no interruptions.

But the idyll would soon be interrupted. Romania entered the war in 1941. Dinu and his future wife, Madeleine Cantacuzino (whom he'd met two years earlier at a musical soirée), went to live in Geneva, where he taught at the conservatory.

The next interruption was illness. He had begun to run a constant fever. Headaches and nausea. There was something wrong with his lungs. In fact, he hadn't felt well since 1943. In 1947 he was diagnosed with Hodgkin's lymphoma. Assisted by injections of cortisone, he continued to record and, when possible, to appear in public. That year he rose to fame with the release of a handful of recordings, including the Schumann Piano Concerto in A Minor conducted by von Karajan.

In the spring of 1948 he again fell gravely ill and began receiving weekly blood transfusions. He had to cancel
most engagements. Concerts abroad were endlessly post-
poned and then abandoned as hopes of recovery dwindled.

After the initial applause that afternoon in Besançon, the
audience held their breath. They had been apprised of his
condition; the atmosphere of tension, the nervous anticipation, was by all accounts excruciating. Lipatti tested the
piano with an ascending scale, his finger collapsing briefly,
to most ears imperceptibly, on the key. Once he finished
the arpeggio, ten seconds of silence – perhaps a moment
of hesitation, or a final summoning of strength – before he
began to play.

Following that initial stumble (edited out in an earlier EMI release), Lipatti lifted off with the first notes of
Bach. Whether his strength was drawn from a short-lived
surge of energy granted by rigorous cortisone treatment
or through some sort of valedictory blaze as he hovered at
death's door, the playing is transcendent. He took his time,
playing the Bach and Mozart pieces more slowly than he
had in June, as if this were the start of his ascension, a final
expansion of the soul.

Defying expectations, he played nearly the entire
programme. Only at the very end did his strength leave
him and he was able to play only thirteen of the fourteen
waltzes, opting instead for a short Bach chorale, 'Jesu, Joy
of Man's Desiring', which he offered after taking a long
break. By the end of the evening, his wife said, he was broken by fatigue and scarcely breathing.

Photographs say as much: in his elegant suit, hair
slicked back, he looks haunted and possessed, his face

ghostly pale, the dark velvety eyes sunk in their sockets. A glass of water, half empty, sits on the piano.

On 2 December, three months after the concert, Dinu Lipatti passed away while listening to Beethoven's String Quartet in F Minor with Madeleine by his side. The immediate cause of death was a ruptured abscess in his only functioning lung. He was thirty-three. After years of separation, his mother, Anna, had been able to defy the repressive laws imposed by the Romanian government and come to see her son at his home in Chêne-Bourg a few months before he died.

Despite years of playing Beethoven, Lipatti never got round to making a recording; he felt he had yet to master the 'Emperor' concerto. Other intended additions to his repertoire, which would have taken him well into 1957, included more Bach, Schubert and Chopin, as well as Stravinsky and Debussy.

He was laid out in the hall of the Geneva Conservatory. Hundreds of people, including Nadia Boulanger, came to bid farewell.

The day after his death the radio broadcast a recording of his final recital, a ghostly transmission from someone who even in life seemed to inhabit a more elevated and ethereal realm. After listening to a recording of that recital of Besançon, even the most secular of us would feel moved to agree with his producer Walter Legge when he said, 'God lent the world His chosen instrument whom we called Dinu Lipatti for too brief a space'.

Where Are You, Patricia Sigl?

(Dispatch from London, Spring 2020)

My street is a quiet one, tucked away in the nether regions of Islington, a few minutes from the canal. Its stillness comes at a price since at any given time there are repairs under way – a window frame, a roof, a facade – and the moment one job is done another springs up a few doors down, turning our street into an open-air workshop. The main movement these days, however, is the come-and-go of delivery vans from Ocado, Iceland and Sainsbury's, and the odd person getting their morning exercise as they shout into their phone. Every now and then an ambulance wails in the distance. One can't ignore the eerie disconnect between the silenced street and the tumult of urgency and emergency elsewhere.

Across the garden from my bedroom looms a giant scaffolding that went up in a noisy burst in early March. There is a limit to how much a family's roof extension can be considered essential, so there it sits, awaiting reactivation. Its tarpaulin flaps at night, its metal frames rattle in the wind, and I often can't help thinking it embodies the country's incomplete standstill. For all the talk of normal life being suspended here, London's lockdown has been somewhat of a sham, and much of business has been allowed to continue as usual. Workers' fates remain at the discretion of their bosses, and many offices, factories and warehouses have not been forced to close.

So far, the UK has the third-highest death toll in the world, numbers still climbing, largely thanks to the government's shambolic planning and indecision and its great reluctance to harm the economy. Its priorities have been made resoundingly clear. Most large construction projects have not been put on hold, and across the city corporate buildings continue their ascension. And not only in the capital: the government recently gave the green light to HS2, a massive rail project connecting London to the north, which will destroy 108 ancient woodlands, taking the birds and bats nesting in its trees. There's not enough money for the NHS, they claim, yet over £115 billion for this ecocidal project.

During the lockdown we contemplate our structures and infrastructures, those greater infrastructures which until now seemed to hold so much of life in place but have collapsed or been put on pause, and the new structures we must create for ourselves in order to give shape and meaning to the days.

On my daily walks I try to vary my circuits. Parallel streets I've never walked, squares I've never crossed. Every action feels like mimesis, an approximation of real life or a weird re-enactment, and walking a bit further than usual, say all the way down to Clerkenwell or the City, seems almost transgressive. Most of the time, I stay within the vague parameters of my neighbourhood. If I turn left onto Gerard Road, I soon arrive at the Pixie house, a tree stump with a door attached to its base, a window overhead and a sign reading PIXIE. Ever since it first appeared a year or two ago I've seen children stop and stare, enchanted, and adults crouching down to take photos. At the moment it seems lived in, no longer part of an imaginary world.

The pixie is in quarantine, behind her closed door and shuttered window. Not long ago, a much more grotesque fairy tale took hold in a large white house around the corner on Colebrooke Row, where Boris Johnson resided during the entire Brexit campaign. Wild promises made, not a single one of the fantasies delivered. A shrugging off of the law seems to linger in the area, mainly in the gardens facing his house, where most people ignore the signs painted on the footpath asking for two-metre distancing and requests to enter the park at one end only. The ribbons of tape strung across benches are also defied; visitors remove them and sit down.

If I turn right outside my house, I soon arrive at St. Peter's Street, which extends from Essex Road down to Noel Road before transforming into Wharf Road at the canal. One street away lives a poet friend, nearly eighty, who hasn't set foot outside for six weeks. He is one of a number of friends over seventy whom I check on regularly, wondering when I shall see them again. The numbers of those felled by the virus in the UK are dizzying, 800 deaths a day, sometimes closer to 900, and, as elsewhere, a vast percentage of them have been elderly.

In the thicket of data, statistics and exponential graphs, in the reports of old people dying abandoned in their flats or in care homes, I seek an individual. And each time I seek one, the face of Patricia Sigl rises to mind. Old, solitary and impoverished, she is the exact sort of person who would get lost in the storm.

I first saw her years ago at the British Library, sitting in a corner of the Rare Books & Music room in front of a mountain of books, her cane propped beside her. Severely hunchbacked, a headscarf tied under her chin, her legs swathed in layers of bandages. At some point I stopped seeing her at the library but began to notice her in my neighbourhood, particularly on St. Peter's Street, always alone, grasping onto railings as she advanced, with a cane and many shopping bags. One evening in late October I glimpsed her outside the local Tesco eating a bag of crisps and went up to say hello. She seemed so surprised that someone was addressing her, I had to repeat my greeting before she swivelled her head to squint up at me with shiny, vivid eyes. I mentioned I would see her at the library. Yes, she said, she used to go there, but it was no longer possible. She then told me she was American, from Wisconsin, and had been living in London since the sixties. Her name was Patricia. Her expression was youthful, her voice almost childlike. She had a PhD in eighteenth-century literature. No friends or family, she added, but many books. She lived in a one-room council flat near Shoreditch. She smiled as she spoke, as if a little astonished to be hearing her own voice.

We form but one layer of existence, one chapter in the history, of a place. I'm reminded of that as I arrive at Camden Passage, a pedestrian strip lined with small shops, restaurants and tea salons, usually interspersed with weekly market stalls selling books and vintage trinkets. With most trade currently suspended, what does 'quotidian' even signify? Now the dimmed shop fronts and absent market stalls represent the shadow selves of human enterprise. At the Camden Head pub only the windows on the top floor, where perhaps the publican lives, remain open. Fifty million pints are threatened to go to waste if the lockdown continues into June, warns the industry.

Camden Passage has been above all the realm of antiquarians, with fourteen shops in the Pierrepont Arcade selling old toys, maps, porcelain, prints, furniture, watches and fountain pens and with an outdoor market on Wednesdays, Saturdays and Sundays. The white indented awning and a string of coloured light bulbs give off the aura of an abandoned seaside pavilion. Without modern-day people populating the passage's little alleys, it is easy to imagine a past reality, almost see the spectres of former traders and those who used the objects now sold as antiques and curiosities. Today I can still see Finbar McDonnell with his long coat and scraggly beard, Angel's longest-standing antiques dealer, who passed away last autumn. A much-loved character in the neighbourhood, he spent pretty much every day of his life in his print shop; it's hard to imagine how he would have endured the quarantine.

There are few antiques to be found at Criterion, the auction house on Essex Road, which usually offers a generous opportunity for window-shopping. The shelves by the window have been emptied and inside only the most unenticing items of furniture remain. All seems quiet at the hundred-year-old funeral parlour further down the street, too. WG MILLER: SUPERIOR FUNERALS, reads the sign, advertising CREMATIONS and EMBALMING. White slatted blinds are drawn against its black lacquer exterior. Most days an array of flower bouquets sits on the pavement outside but today there's only a fern-like plant called mother-in-law's tongue in the window, and a man in a cap adding a fresh layer of paint to the sill. Funerals have recently been limited to close family, with some directors suggesting live-streaming of burials.

Glimpses of an afterlife are more visible at Get Stuffed, the taxidermy shop on the corner, where the stiff dogs in the display have been given white face masks. The more exotic species dwell at the rear of the shop, unmasked and in the shadows, pretty much emblematic of the animal kingdom's current predicament. Since the lockdown began, people around the world have been commenting on how close they feel to nature, how reconnected to all the flora and fauna. I too have revelled in entrancing images of animals reclaiming urban space, including photographs of a herd of deer lolling about in a garden in East London and the splendid white shaggy goats roaming the streets of Llandudno. Yet my feeling of connection to nature has mostly taken on another shape, more tortured and abstract. I think instead about the bats and other live animals in the wet markets in China (and Indonesia) and the cosmic scale of their suffering. The exact origin of this virus has yet to be confirmed but there is no doubt these markets are hubs of cruelty and disease, and I fervently hope this pandemic will bring the consumption of wildlife to an end.

Yet I try not to let the news completely invade my mental space, and work on my novel. Is it still relevant? Does it matter? Well, it happens to feature two people sequestered from the outside world. And bats. I work at my desk, in the company of my cat, books and life decisions. Often I despair at being so far from my parents in Mexico and my sister and niece in New York. We've been keeping a chronicle in four voices, A Tale of Three Cities, charting the unfolding horror and incompetent leadership in each of our countries. There's no guarantee of a flight between London and Mexico City, and I can't help asking myself how I ended up so far from my family and origins. My second encounter with Patricia Sigl was again at dusk, on the corner of St. Peter's and Devonia. Upon spotting her hunched silhouette, I called out her name. She seemed to recognise my voice before she was able to see my face, again swivelling her head around and tilting it upwards – Chloe, right?

She held on to a nearby railing, never loosening her grip of her collection of shopping bags, as we stood and chatted. She told me she was managing despite her ailments, and was much more interested in talking about her PhD at the University of Wales on an eighteenth-century playwright named Elizabeth Inchbald whom no one ever read anymore. I tried to imagine the path from scholarship to such poverty and promised myself that the next time I saw her I would invite her to tea at a pub or café nearby.

Islington is one of the most diverse boroughs in London, half of its homes privately owned or rented, and half council housing. My street is pretty much split down the middle. The people who have lived here the longest congregate on the pavement, sitting on their steps with cigarettes and cups of tea, a familiarity that extends to the street, they know each other and chat, while most of the private owners withdraw behind their renovated facades. Only the 8 o'clock clap for the NHS every Thursday night brings everyone together, a rare moment of communion, when faces appear at windows and doorways to cheer on our beleaguered healthcare system.

During lockdown we are forced to revisit all the decisions we have made in life, and so must this government. Starved by a decade of Tory austerity, the NHS is understaffed and underfunded and in total disarray. There are also constant reminders of the staggering folly that is Brexit, its idiocy put further on display as the UK missed out on an EU ventilator scheme and PPE distribution, and British doctors and nurses were pulled out of retirement to make up for the shortage of NHS staff after many of the European nurses and doctors lost their right to remain. One can only hope that Boris Johnson, having recovered from Covid-19 himself and now singing the glories of the NHS, with particular praise for the two foreign nurses who didn't leave his bedside while he was in intensive care, will do far more to guarantee its survival. One hopes he will no longer miss emergency COBRA meetings to address the pandemic. One hopes the British media, until now complacent to the point of complicity, can finally bring itself to hold the government accountable for the unfolding catastrophe. One hopes.

It was the NHS surgery on St. Peter's Street that Patricia Sigl would visit regularly, and during these days of crisis I scan the street for a hunched silhouette. It's been several months since I last saw her. I wonder how she is weathering the lockdown. Who checks in on her, who brings her food. Well, the truth is I wonder whether she is still alive. Was she one of the 843 who perished on 25 April or one of the 686 on 12 April? Or perhaps, like Finbar McDonnell, she mercifully passed away before the nightmare began. Some day, when this crisis is over, I may come across an early edition of Elizabeth Inchbald at one of the antiquarian stalls in Camden Passage, inscribed by a 'Miss Patricia

Sigl, an American resident in London, authority on the eighteenth-century theatre', as I once saw her referred to in a footnote. When this is over, there will be far too many footnotes.

Thinking Green: Petra Kelly

Few details of the death of Petra Kelly are more symbolic than the word *must* interrupted. When policemen entered her house in Bonn after relatives raised the alarm, they discovered two bodies decomposed beyond recognition. Accompanying the gruesome scenario was the ominous hum of an electric typewriter that had been left running for nearly three weeks. In the carriage lay a sheet of paper on which Petra's partner, Gert Bastian, had been writing a letter to his lawyer. Halfway through the word *müssen* he was interrupted, and only got as far as 'müs'. Petra's brief life – driven by a sense of duty, urgency, powered by a constant feeling of 'must', haunted by the thought she was never doing enough – could be summed up in this truncated word.

She was only forty-four when she died, in October 1992, and her murder sent shock waves throughout the world. As co-founder of the German Green Party she had been their most visible face. Her causes were manifold – nuclear disarmament, indigenous rights, women's rights, sustainable development, demilitarisation, democratisation of the Soviet bloc, Tibet – and she did what she could to introduce them into government policy. Yet it wasn't easy being a female politician, and her fervour was often mocked by the opposition. At the Bundestag, where she held a parliamentary seat from 1983 to 1990, microphones were permanently tuned to a man's voice, rendering a woman's voice unnaturally shrill; only after some campaigning were they returned to default mode each time a woman spoke.

Aware of the perils of a coalition government, Petra Kelly warned the Greens of the dangers of compromise and shared power. Non-violent civil disobedience was her preferred weapon, and even when she was a member of parliament she'd protest outside the building. Over the years her stance isolated her; some later argued that her modest existence and abandonment by the Greens made her vulnerable and exposed.

To this day, the circumstances of her death, and Bastian's, remain a mystery. Police found Petra in bed with a bullet to her temple and him in the corridor with a bullet to his forehead, his gun lying on the floor nearby. Most concluded she was murdered by Bastian, a retired army general twenty-five years her senior. Others blamed a politically motivated third party – their alarm system had been switched off, the balcony door unlocked. Whatever the truth, the Bonn police closed the investigation within twenty-four hours.

Two years after her death a collection of Petra Kelly's writings, *Thinking Green! Essays on Environmentalism, Feminism and Nonviolence*, was published. It is a powerful summons beyond the grave. Each chapter was a call to arms, covering most subjects that were dear to her, fuelled by a hope that would be much harder to conjure up in the present. 'Green politics must address the spiritual vacuum of industrial society,' she wrote. The cover photograph shows Petra in a helmet decked in yellow flowers, yet her smiling face doesn't hide the fatigue. The dark circles under her eyes betrayed a chronic kidney disorder but also a restlessness and exhaustion, her anxiety for the planet internalised. In her last interview, she said, 'Everything we do is like the labour of Sisyphus'; the defiant mythical rock and the stones in Petra's kidneys like some sort of nominative determinism.

My family met her in 1991 in Morelia, Mexico, where my parents had organised a symposium for writers and environmentalists. Petra immediately stood out – magnetic, valiant, intense – and we stayed in touch afterwards via her beloved fax machine. In a strange twist of fate, my parents had lunch scheduled with her in Bonn the day after their bodies were discovered and had been trying to call the house for weeks. Months later they received a package in the post, sent by Joschka Fischer: a carved wooden fish Petra had been planning to give them.

The battles to be fought today feel even more urgent and doom-laden than those of the seventies and eighties, though many of them alas remain the same. Petra Kelly couldn't have been more prescient when she said of the challenges facing this century: 'If we don't do the impossible, we shall be faced with the unthinkable.'

A Brief History
of the World

1

It all started with a minuscule green flare in the sky that
after wandering the universe and finding no corner in
which to dwell collected enough star dust to grow into a
tiny comet which then landed in Earth's ocean and after a
few days, nourished by salt water, exploded into tiny particles and each of these particles grew a webbed foot, and
then several more, followed by a rubbery body and a pair
of round eyes. And the ocean, sensing a new presence of
life and happy to finally have company, adjusted its temperature to make itself more welcoming.

2

The Reign of the Axolotl, ancient salamanders – amphib-
ians native to the canals of Xochimilco in Mexico City –
begins. Axolotls are able to regrow severed limbs and
retain their infant features throughout their lives, never

undergoing metamorphosis; therefore all appear to be the same age and there is no hierarchy within their society. They are peaceful but lack assertive personalities, and as the world expands and more species come into existence, the axolotls are eventually replaced by the Feathered Serpent Quetzalcóatl, God of Wind and Wisdom, who reigns harmoniously.

3

A solar eclipse unbalances the cosmological order, Quetzalcóatl is dethroned and a kingdom of shadows is established. This long night leads to the Reign of Quetzalcóatl's brother Tezcatlipoca, Smoking Mirror. Rivalry grows among the Aztec gods until they hand over earthly matters to man: Moctezuma is made emperor. The Spaniards arrive by sea, Moctezuma taken prisoner in his own palace. He is visited by Huitzilopochtli, god of war, as a hummingbird, who tells him the invading men are not gods and gives him a secret weapon. A bloody battle ensues. Defying all expectations, the Aztecs prevail and the Spaniards are defeated.

4

In an obsidian mirror in Moctezuma's palace, an Aztec priestess glimpses scenes from past centuries elsewhere in the world. In ancient Greece, people gather in a planetarium and dream of reaching the stars. Enormous water-powered machines in the shape of dragons are installed on rivers in Tang dynasty China. Somewhere on the Indian subcontinent, a species of macaque establishes control over all the temples but continues the practice of Buddhism. Women and children build two visions of paradise on earth: Petra and Palmyra. Hundreds of thousands of migrating humpback whales sing and breach.

5

A mysterious epidemic has toppled the Roman Empire, felling its highest officials. Mass poisoning is suspected. In the Middle Ages, a disastrous plague, spread by giant spiders, sweeps the European continent. The spiders are finally wiped out by resilient cats brought over from Egypt. Tamed gargoyles help to erect grand cathedrals while monasteries fill up with anatomists of melancholy and the convents with female scribes. A new type of candle is invented that burns for fifty-five hours, leading to widespread insomnia. Herds of elephants and prides of lions roam the African continent, crowding out the human population.

6

The Aztecs set sail for Europe on the Spanish boats that weren't burned by Cortés, manned by conquistador slaves. The ships land at Palos de la Frontera and a war of religion ensues. The Virgin Mary is supplanted by Our Mother Tonantzin, maize replaces wheat as a staple, cocoa beans become the most valued currency. Madrid is the Aztec capital in Spain, but the human sacrifice required to honour and appease the gods is carried out at the Alhambra in Granada. The Aztecs are unable to extend their influence further into Europe as they can't make it across the Pyrenees.

7

An enormous meteorite falls into the Zone of Silence, a mysterious part of the Mexican desert. All the principal Aztec priests travel to visit the crater; as they stand inspecting it, another huge meteorite falls and crushes them. The populace is freed; no more human sacrifice. Under the mantle of black dust that now enshrouds the country, the Spanish slaves revolt and spread Christianity. Meanwhile, Berber hordes paddle across the Strait of Gibraltar and wrest Spain from the Aztecs. Everywhere people are reading the newly invented printed books. An unknown breed of sea monster is spotted in the Pacific Ocean.

8

In Renaissance Italy, an artist draws a perfect circle while pigeons invade the town squares before moving on to Constantinople. Wooden flying machines are tried out, unsuccessfully, from rooftops, causing dozens of deaths. In Germany, the Jesuit scholar Athanasius Kircher unsettles his fellow believers by casting demons on the wall with the help of a magic lantern. And thanks to Galileo and his telescope, mountains are discovered on the moon, unleashing a craze in the study of lunar topography. Astronomers are astonished to find that the moon is in fact the head of the dismembered Mexican goddess Coyolxauhqui.

9

After a violent storm a series of dams bursts in seventeenth-century Holland, submerging its affluence under massive floods; entire communities migrate to the upper storeys of windmills, and the country's most famous optics laboratory is inundated. From the small population of Sephardic Jews is born a new language, Hebrish, a combination of Hebrew and Flemish. Magnitude 9 earthquakes along the entire Eastern Pacific trigger a gigantic tsunami; the sea recoils and rushes back, devouring all life and construction in its path. In Britain, King Charles I and his army prevail, Oliver Cromwell is beheaded and there is rejoicing in Ireland.

10

In Russia, Catherine the Great builds her Amber Room; two wolfhounds from the palace get trapped in the amber and until they are freed the country is declared in a state of emergency. Much of Europe is overtaken by carnivals; masked orgies and incessant feasting fuel fantasies of inverting the established order. The Spanish botanist José Celestino Mutis's widely circulated book about the dreams of plants triggers a small epidemic of mental disturbances. Alexander von Humboldt visits Mexico and after becoming attached to the volcano Iztaccihuatl, 'White Woman' in Nahuatl, decides to reside permanently on her slopes.

II

On the eastern coast of the thirteen British colonies, American patriots revolt against foreign rule. During the Boston Tea Party, an entire shipment of chests of tea is dumped into the harbour, creating new breeds of over-caffeinated, electrified fish that rapidly grow in size and leap out of the water to bite British soldiers, drawn to the red of their uniforms. The Atlantic cod, bluefish and black sea bass are found to be particularly aggressive. Iroquois, Algonquian, Wampanoag, Powhatan, Lenni-Lenape and other Indian tribes fight alongside the Patriots and independence is won. Tribal delegates take part in the Continental Congress.

12

In France it is the era of the hot-air balloon, or *montgolfière*, enthusiasts: Louis XVI sets his sights on the sky, hoping to expand his kingdom. All ascents are cut short by the French Revolution. The *sans-culottes* attack statues; to their surprise, certain statues fight back. The female knitters seated at the foot of the guillotine are found to be knitting back to life the cats killed in the 1730s cat massacre. Marie Antoinette escapes execution but is to be kept as a permanent exhibit in the former tiger enclosure at the Jardin des Plantes.

13

War breaks out between China and Japan over contested territory as well as claims to a rare species of dark blue nightingale said to summer in China and winter in the forests of Japan; for both countries, it is a national symbol. The war rages on for nearly two decades. After a year of deadlock, both sides back down and once they do, they realise that as a result of all the warfare, the fragile nightingale has gone extinct. Learning of the tragic loss, Maya in Mexico send flocks of resplendent quetzals to both countries.

14

The Industrial Revolution spreads across Europe. Thanks to the telegraph, occasional signals are picked up of ancient gods sending messages, but no one can interpret them. Women no longer work at the loom but receive equal wages to men in textile mills. An entrepreneurial Italian designs a tall, commanding puppet. For a brief time, this gives way to the Reign of Puppets. They supervise factories, drive steam engines, develop an obsession with cotton. The puppets are known to mistreat the children working for them. In a small town in Germany these conditions lead to the Children's Rebellion.

15

Dozens of broad boulevards are laid out in nineteenth-century Paris during the renovation of the city. Congeries of spectres are released when the grounds are dug up and certain buildings demolished; the population more than triples. Mediums hold cabinet positions in the government and important matters are decided by tabletop conversations with spirits. Hurricane-force winds batter Patagonia, carrying thousands of feathers from Antarctic penguins to southernmost Chile and Argentina. Hieroglyphs on the Rosetta Stone are deciphered, yielding an account of attacks by Nile hippopotami and remedies for hippo bites.

16

Napoleon III sends Maximilian of Austria to become Emperor of Mexico. During a visit to Yucatán, which is suffering a drought, Maximilian is pushed into the cenote at Chichén Itzá to appease the Mayan rain god, Chaac. Empress Carlota assumes his place, but grief drives her to madness; among her many follies, she endeavours to recreate Miramare, their castle in Trieste, on the coast of Veracruz. After a year she is deposed by freemasons and ransomed by her brother Leopold II of Belgium. She spends her days in Bouchout Castle, holding long conversations with her pet armadillo.

17

After a thirty-five-year-long dictatorship, Porfirio Díaz is ousted from power and immured in the Cananea copper mine; Francisco Madero seizes the presidency, setting off the Mexican Revolution. Revolutionaries across the land are assisted by armies of feral dogs, descendants of mastiffs and wolfhounds brought to the New World by Spanish conquistadors to attack and devour Indians, that have banded together to help overthrow feudal rule. A battalion of young girls under twelve-year-old Lupita Pérez joins Emiliano Zapata and victory follows victory. Lupita saves Zapata from an assassin's bullet and he becomes president. He distributes all the haciendas to landless peasants.

18

Sailors on the battleship *Potemkin*, enraged at the sight of prams tumbling down the Odessa Steps, fight their way past Cossacks to Tsar Nicholas II's palace and force-feed the royal family rotten fish. The Romanovs are imprisoned but rescued by a rain of wolves that descends moments before their planned execution. The family is granted asylum in Mexico, and sails before the revolutionaries can change their minds. Following Rasputin's murder, fortune-tellers exert their power over villages and twelve years of fighting ensue. Stalin dies leading the failed Kerensky Offensive, and with Lenin's support, Trotsky becomes head of Soviet Russia.

19

The Austro-Hungarian Empire has crumbled. Skies are permanently overcast and a group of former ministers is seen in a field doing the Dance of Death. Among the twelve states carved out of the defunct empire is Sintirom, a homeland where Romani people can wander at will. Rabid speculation in cocoa bean futures precipitates a worldwide stock market crash and a return to gold as the principal currency. Radio listeners in Spain, Italy and Germany are hypnotised by the voices of fascist dictators. Yeti yak herders are spotted in the Himalayas while a Sasquatch tribe migrates north to the Arctic tundra.

20

In the early 1940s mass extermination of Jews is averted just in time by the appearance of the Golem. The towering clay figure makes a dramatic return, resurrected by Jewish mystics in order to save their people. He appears in Prague, and after single-handedly vanquishing Nazi troops at the border he marches into Germany, unsealing the ghettos and smashing fascists with his fists. Once his people are out of danger, and their dignity reinstated, he collapses into the mud, vanishing without a trace.

21

At the height of the Cold War, an unprecedented number of birds are registered in both halves of Berlin, due to a high demand for passenger pigeons. A spy at the Sugar Research Foundation releases a secret study about sugar's role in heart disease; sugar is banned in the United States, Cuba falls to Fidel Castro. The United States and the USSR argue over the laws of outer space – the legal status of cosmonauts, canines and launched objects – but these remain too abstract to enforce. Mao Zedong drowns while swimming in the Yangtze River, after colliding with a baiji.

22

Humankind finally recognises that animals have figured at every stage of human history. Unprecedented concern for animal welfare overspreads the globe. Poachers are imprisoned throughout Africa. A new generation of doctors in China debunks the myths of traditional Chinese medicine, slashing the demand for tiger parts, seahorses, totoaba swim bladders and rhinoceros horns. Factory farming is banned and slaughterhouses are slowly phased out in Europe and the United States – battles are still being fought elsewhere. The Japanese government shuts down the dolphin drive hunt at Taiji and outlaws whaling. The United Nations issues a ten-year moratorium on ocean fishing.

23

In Russia a famous troupe of clowns has taken control of the government. All circus bears are released but asked to report back should their advice be needed. Trade tensions erupt with Poland and Hungary over a new export tax on pickles and dessert wines. The country's two most accomplished female mathematicians defect during a world tournament in Iceland. Relations with the rest of the world depend on the outcome of an ongoing game of chess.

Along the US-Mexican border, gangs of narcosatanists are dismembering young women. The murders, shrouded in mystery, have been impossible to stop – until a female army of Tzitzimimes intervenes, with the help of migratory jaguars. The Tzitzimimes, or monsters of twilight, is also the name of an all-girl rock band that has mesmerised Mexico. Meanwhile, the axolotls in Xochimilco continue to worship their ancient deity, the Supreme Axolotl, knowing that all history is circular; they sense a coming cosmic crisis and are hatching a plan, growing new limbs and preparing for a novel planetary order. The world turns on its axis.

Note on the Text

Many of the texts included in this collection were originally published or broadcast in the following places:

'Faits Divers' in *mirrorcity* (Hayward Gallery, 2014); 'Pigeon' in *Litro* (2014); 'A Celebration of the Circus Flea' in *Science & Fiction* (RCA/Black Dog Publishing, 2014); 'The Kafka Society' in *The Liberal* (2005); 'World Weather Report' is excerpted from the text 'Notes on the Weather' in *Lucifer over London* (Influx Press, 2014); 'Into the Cosmos' (2012) and 'Kopfkino' (2013) in *Granta* online and 'The Tension of Transience' in *Granta* (2019); 'Hymn to the Stray Dog' in *LitHub* (2019); 'Baroque' on BBC Radio 4 (2013); '15 Moments of Lightness in *Fanny and Alexander*' (2020), 'Varieties of Exile: Mavis Gallant' (2019), 'Tea and Creatures with Leonora Carrington' (2017) and 'Petra Kelly' [Thinking Green: Petra Kelly] (2019) in *frieze*; 'In the Laboratory: Aby Warburg' (2020) and 'The Allure of the Analogue' (2022) in the *London Review of Books* and 'A Leonora Carrington A–Z' on the *London Review of Books* website (2017); 'Beatrice Hastings' [I Am Many: Beatrice Hastings] in *Tate, Etc* (2017); a version of 'Last Recital: Dinu Lipatti' in *The Threepenny Review* (2009); a version of 'A Life Remembered: Chiki Weisz' in *Habitus* (2010);

'Uprooted: Encounters Between Mexican Flora and Its Foreigners' in *MAL* (2019); 'Map of a Lost Soul' in *Where You Are* (Visual Editions, 2013); and 'Where Are You, Patricia Sigl?' in *n+1* (2020).

Thanks and Acknowledgements

I decided to title this collection after a story I wrote in Berlin, the city where I became a writer (starting with my first published tale, 'The Kafka Society', in 2005). Each time I sit down to write, I return. I dedicate this book to my dear friends from those days, with whom I continue the dialogue today: Tania Hron, Helga von Kügelgen and Ursula Tax. Mathilde Bonnefoy and Dirk Wilutzky. Signe Rossbach, Christina Dimitriadis and the Marashian family.

And of course to my own extraordinary family, who are present in everything I write.

Immense gratitude to Gareth Evans and Jessica Chandler of House Sparrow Press, who had the idea for this collection, and for helping create, with the talented hand of Theo Inglis, such a beautiful edition.

Great thanks to Alicia Kroell at Catapult for granting the book a second life, and to Sarah Jean Grimm and Wah-Ming Chang.

There are too many beloved friends in England to thank, but you know who you are. I would like to single out two: Devorah Baum, whose wisdom buoys up the days, and Julian Sands, whose remarkable spirit will continue to inspire those of us who had the fortune to know him.

CHLOE ARIDJIS is a Mexican American writer based in London. She is the author of three novels: *Book of Clouds*, which won the Prix du Premier Roman Étranger in France; *Asunder*, set in London's National Gallery; and *Sea Monsters*, awarded the 2020 PEN/Faulkner Award for Fiction. Aridjis has written for various art journals and was guest curator of the Leonora Carrington exhibition at Tate Liverpool. She was awarded a Guggenheim Fellowship in 2014 and the Eccles Centre & Hay Festival Writers Award in 2020. Aridjis is a founding member of XR Writers Rebel, a group of writers who focus on addressing biodiversity loss and the climate emergency: www.writersrebel.com.